# Urban Productive Safety Net Programme Impact on Livelihood

# Urban Productive Safety Net Programme Impact on Livelihood

Dr. Karanam Viswa Bhushan

GenNext Publication

First Published, 2021

*Published by*

GenNext Publication
5, Ansari Road
Daryaganj, New Delhi-110002
Phone: 9811692060
E-mail: gennextpublication@hotmail.com

*Printed at:* Gyan Press, Delhi.

**Cataloging in Publication Data—DK**
Courtesy: D.K. Agencies (P) Ltd. <docinfo@dkagencies.com>

**Bhushan, Karanam Viswa,** 1963- **author.**
Urban Productive Safety Net Programme impact on livelihood / Dr. Karanam Viswa Bhushan.
pages cm
Includes bibliographical references.
ISBN 9789353243241 (HB)
"An Imprint of Kalpaz Publication"

1. Urban Productive Safety Net Programme (Ethiopia). 2. Poverty—Prevention—Government policy—Ethiopia—Dire Dawa. 3. Urban poor—Government policy—Ethiopia—Dire Dawa. I. Title.

LCC HC845.Z9P6 2021 | DDC 362.50963 23

# Contents

*Acknowledgements* ..... 7
*List of Tables* ..... 9
*List of Figures* ..... 11

1. Introduction ..... 13
2. Literature Review ..... 23
3. Research Methodology ..... 45
4. Results and Discussions ..... 55
5. Conclusions and Recommendations ..... 91

*Reference* ..... 95
*List of Acronyms* ..... 99
*Index* ..... 101

# Acknowledgements

I would like to thank and praise the Almighty God.

It is my pleasure to extend my thanks to my student, Hilina Tessema for her contribution and sincere involvement.

I am ever grateful to all those who had helped me and willingly participated in my research work by providing me very essential information for my research work and for book publication.

I would like to express my heartfelt gratitude for my beloved twin brother Rev. Fr. Dhaman Kumar. MSFS for his moral support and encouragement.

# List of Tables


Table 3.1: Sample Size Allocation per Kebele and Beneficiary Type ................. 51
Table 4.1: Socio Demographic Characteristics of Respondents .......................... 55
Table 4.2: Marital Status and Sex of Households by Type of Beneficiary .......... 58
Table 4.3: No of Family Members in the Household ......................................... 59
Table 4.4: Health status of the Household Member ........................................... 60
Table 4.5: Beneficiaries Satisfaction in Targeting ............................................... 61
Table 4.6: Beneficiaries Satisfaction in Support Appropriateness ........................ 64
Table 4.7: Beneficiaries Satisfaction in Timeliness of Cash Transfer .................. 65
Table 4.8: Effects of UPSNP ................................................................................ 66
Table 4.9: Household Level of Literacy ............................................................... 71
Table 4.10: Respondents' Means of Livelihoods .................................................. 79
Table 4.11: No of UPSNP Beneficiaries in the Household .................................. 81
Table 4.12: Major Expenses of the Household ..................................................... 82
Table 4.13: Beneficiary Type and the Food Access Status ................................... 86
Table 4.14: Challenges in the Urban Productive Safety Net Programme Implementation ....................................................................... 89

# List of Figures

Figure 2.1: Sustainable Livelihoods Framework. Graph from DFID (1999) ........40
Figure 2.2: Conceptual Framework of the Study ........42
Figure 3.1: Map of Dire Dawa City Administration by Sample ........46
Figure 4.1: Educational Levels of the Household Head. ........57
Figure 4.2: Income Status of the HH after joining UPSNP ........84
Figure 4.3 Households Number of Meals Taken Per Day. ........85

## Chapter One

# Introduction

### 1.1 Background of the Study

Social protection generally encompasses social and economic transfers, access to services, social support and care services, and equity and non-discrimination legislation and policies. In this regards, different nations around the globe have been designing numerous social protection policies and have been implementing in order to achieve the mentioned targets of social protection. In this regards, productive safety net is one component of the social protection designed to support the poor and reduce vulnerability in Ethiopia (MOLSA, 2014).

A number of countries have implemented safety net schemes to tackle the food crisis. In less developed countries, the poor rely for their food security on government safety nets. Bangladesh moved food supplies from subsidized sales channels to food transfers linked to specific schemes targeting specific groups of households in the early 1990s.Other essential transfer programmes are the vulnerable group Development programme which is targeted at poor women which offers 2 years of monthly food rationing. Vulnerable group feeding is a recovery system designed to help the vulnerable through natural disasters. Since1997 India has been eligible for food subsidies. The Subsidies rely on whether families are listed as above poverty line, below poverty line, or poorest of the poor. In addition to the in-kind food support, India has a cash transfer scheme called the National Rural Employment Guarantee Act in the form of public services. The programme restricted to rural areas, is not directly targeted, but operates through the collection of the vulnerable for them. In addition, the rice subsidy programme is one of Indonesia's several mutual assistance and safety net programmes. There are several different services, such as cash transfers from poor households to public school students and cash transfers to older people, disabled people and young people (Jha, Kotwal, & Ramaswami, 2013).

A great part of the information about the long term effects of cash transfer and other social help programmes originates from Latin America, fundamentally Mexico and Brazil(Marston & Grady, 2014).During the 1980s, Latin America endured the most serious emergency in its history. To help address the emergency, the International Monetary Fund (IMF) and the World Bank proposed and financed auxiliary modification and adjustment programmes all through the region to address the vulnerabilities of poor people, and also during the Mexican crisis (Tequila crisis) the first conditional cash transfer programme started in Brazil in 1995 which now expanded in many countries(WB, 1996).

Ethiopia is taken as economically fast growing country in the Sub Saharan African region, where headcount poverty has declined by around 93 percent over the past fifteen years from 45.5 percent in 2000 to 23.5 percent in 2016(UNDP Ethiopia, 2018). According to the recent report of the Household Consumption Expenditure Survey, about 5.3 million people are lifted out of poverty between 2010/11 and 2015/16.Deprivation gap and measures of intensity of deprivation decreased from 10.1% and 3.9% in 2000 to 3.7% and 1.4% in 2016, respectively. Nevertheless, poverty in Ethiopia remains a problem as more than 22 million people live below the national poverty line. Poverty is predominantly a rural phenomenon in Ethiopia, while urban headcount poverty decreased from 36.9% in 2000 to 14.8% in 2016; rural poverty declined in the same period from 45.4% to 25.6%.The government is also implementing a huge social protection programme to help the poor maintaining their livelihood. The Productive Safety Net Programme (PSNP) is the largest social protection programme in Africa which support close to 8 million chronically food insecure people and it has been implemented since 2005(UNDP Ethiopia, 2018).

Promoting productive safety net is one of the focus areas of Ethiopian National Social Protection Policy. The productive safety net programme was designed to be based on the establishment and implementation of strategies to address people in social problems. In general, to support the poor and reduce vulnerability, productive safety net programme are designed in the rural and urban areas (MOLSA, 2014). Ethiopia's Productive Safety Net Programme (PSNP), which essentially gives cash transfer and some nourishment help, is the biggest of its sort in Africa. It is additionally among the world's biggest social help programmes (Marston & Grady, 2014).

To address the poorest and vulnerable segment of the urban population, Ethiopian government designed the Urban Productive Safety Net Programme (UPSNP) for five years (2016/17-2020/21). As a pilot project, it has started its implementation in 11 major cities with intervention on 604,000 beneficiaries in the first phase. The 11 major cities include; the two City Administrations (Addis Ababa and Dire Dawa), and one major city/town from the nine regional states each. These are Adama (Oromia), Assaita (Afar), Asosa (Benshangul), Dessie (Amhara), Gambella (Gambella), Hawassa (SNNPR), Harar (Harari), Jigjiga (Somali), and

Mekele (Tigray) in collaboration with the World Bank and other stakeholders. The long-term programme framework has an objective of reaching 4.7 million poor in 972 urban areas (MoUDH, 2016).

UPSNP implementation started to gain focus of various scholars, policy makers and other stakeholders on the impacts of the programme on reaching the expected and targeted outcomes. In concomitant to this, few studies and reports have tried to probe into the programmes'-effect on various aspects of the target outcomes. Livelihoods improvement is one of the major parts in the safety net programme and a great emphasis has been laid on livelihoods component as its ability to curtail the vicious circle of poverty and enhance wellbeing of urban households is deemed to be high. Cognizant to this, the main goal of this study is to assess the improvement that UPSNP brought on the livelihoods of households with a special emphasis on the urban poor in Dire Dawa City Administration.

## 1.2 Problem Statement

In attempting to tackle the problems of urban poverty, large aggregation of results have failed to see and have overlooked issues; inter alia: the agglomerated locations of poor in a city, differences between poor areas within cities, in seeing whether access to services among differing subgroups, whether targeted programmes really are reaching the poorest of the poor and the vulnerable, and also failed to formulate effective poverty reduction policies and programmes (Baker & Schuler, 2004). Although these are not the domains of this particular study, the thematic issues raised bring critical components on what to look for when assessing the UPSN programme of Ethiopia in a specific location, like that of Dire Dawa City.

According to CSA (2011), poverty rate has declined to 29.6 percent (30.4% in rural and 25.7% in urban areas) although, 23.5 percent of total populations (25.6% in rural and 14.8% in urban areas) were still found to be under the poverty line in 2015/16. Similarly, the poverty rate of Dire Dawa Administration was found to be 33.1% in 1999/00 and it slightly increased to 35.2% in 2004/05, although it decreased to 28.3% in 2010/11; while the 2015/16 survey based analysis shows that the poverty rate of the region has further declined to 15.4 percent (CSA, 2018).In line with its positive advancement, the Government of Ethiopia is still further contributing intensely to lessen destitution and advance social improvement. Among the poverty reduction programmes implemented by the Government of Ethiopia, the Productive Safety Net Programme is one of the huge social protection programmes designed to help the poor in maintaining their livelihoods and betterment of their overall welfare (UNDP Ethiopia, 2018).

The government has started social protection programmes to enable the poor and to keep up some base degree of living standard the poor. Although greater focus was given the rural safety net, – which by in large considering the greater concentration of population in rural areas as a plausible initiative -the government has additionally begun executing urban safety net programme, which relied upon the notion of the reduction of neediness further and bridging the gap in the welfare of the poor in all parts of the nation (UNDP, 2018).

In line to this, urbanization and the high influx of rural to urban migration have intensified poverty of the urban population in many cities. Dire Dawa as the second largest city in Ethiopia with a rapid urban growth; faces many urbanization related challenges including periodical floods entering the city from the north, which affect majority of the population living in the slums or substandard housing, making the entire the river side area vulnerable to floods, informal settlements, lacks access to clean water, proper sanitation and etc. In 1995 the number of population in Dire Dawa was 180, 000 continuously growing to 229,000 in 2000 with a rate of 27 percent, and further growing to 284,000 in 2005 with a rate of 24 percent. Further growth was also anticipated in 2015 (UN Habitat, 2008).

In addition to the severe living conditions and inaccessibility of basic facilities such as health and education among the urban poor, the problem of food insecurity in the urban settings is getting chronic and highly complex. To alleviate urban food insecurity and to tackle the increased level of vulnerability, the Ethiopian Government developed Urban Food Security Strategy and Urban Job Creation and Food Security Programme. Few of the root causes of food insecurity in urban areas include: unsystematic rural-urban migration (that is migration which is not guided by economic indicators), lack of adequate employment opportunities, lack of integrated social protection for disadvantaged groups, underutilized potential of urban agriculture, lack of modern market exchange system, lack of efficient service delivery, lack of conducive working environment in the rural areas which force the youth to migrate to urban areas, poor solid and liquid waste management; and environmental, natural and man-made hazards. To respond to most of the aforementioned causes and to intervene in a right manner, UPSNP has been initiated by the government as an instrument to implement Urban Food Security Strategy (MoUDH, 2016).

Plethora studies have also been conducted concerning the rural settings of the Productive safety Net Programme in Ethiopia. Most studies focused on households' food security, asset accumulation, asset ownership, situation of poverty, practice and challenges of the programme. Although most focus and greater emphasis was given to the rural PSNP, which by in large considering the urban-rural population ratio is plausible to emphasize on the rural setting, yet this study focuses on the urban PSNP and allied issues as there still remains a great scope for addressing the much needed targets of UPSNP in cities like Dire Dawa in relatation to urban poverty and livelihoods. In concomitant to this, the livelihood component which is introduced in the PSNP is a new component, and this study is deemed to bring significant implications to the programme's implementation in this regards.

## 1.3 Objectives of the study

### *1.3.1 General Objective of the Study*

The overarching objective of this study is to assess the contribution of Urban Productive Safety Net Programme to households' livelihood improvement in Dire Dawa City Administration.

### *1.3.2 Specific Objective of the Study*

The study has the following specific objectives,

1) To assess perceptions of beneficiaries towards the implementation and overall benefits of the programme
(2) To examine the contribution of UPSNP to households' livelihoods and food access in the study area, and
(3) To identify the challenges which influence the effective implementation of UPSNP in Dire Dawa City Administration

## 1.4 Research Questions

In response to the above stated objectives, the study attempt to answer the following research questions

(1) What are the beneficiaries' perceptions towards implementation and benefits of the programme?
(2) What are the major contributions of UPSNP to households' livelihoods?
(3) How is UPSNP helping household build their assets?
(4) What is the role of UPSNP in the improvements of households' food access?
(5) Is the programme being implemented as strategized initially by following all the necessary targeting, re-targeting, payment processes and complaints and grievance redressing criterion set in Dire Dawa City?
(6) What are the implementation challenges of UPSNP in Dire Dawa City Administration?

## 1.5 Significance of the study

The study provides important information regarding the contribution of Urban Productive Safety Net Programme to households' livelihood improvement. The findings will help the City Administration and all concerned bodies involved in the programme implementation to explore possible ideas, techniques and strategies that can improve the proper implementation of the programme. Besides, the study can be useful as a reference material for academic researchers and scholars who are interested in a further scrutiny regarding the programme and related activities. Furthermore, the results of the study may benefit, the researcher as well as the larger beneficiary community, in that it can provide access to a wide range of evidences about programme's implementation and its real impacts on lives of the poor.

## 1.6 Scope and Limitations of the Study

The scope of the study is delimited to the boundary of Dire

Dawa City Administration, with focuses only on Kebele 05, 08 and 09. The study area is selected purposively because the programme first started its implementation on those Kebeles and Ketenas were selected randomly. The study considers both conditional cash transfers and unconditional cash transfer beneficiaries from each Ketena. The study covers a time frame between 2017 and 2019 for assessing the programme's implementation and to assess the changes in beneficiaries' livelihoods status. The thematic scope of the study is bounded on perceptions of beneficiaries towards the programme, the contributions of the programme to households' livelihood and food access status, and challenges of programme implementation. Plus, the study only focused on limited aspects of the implementation spot check assessment as some components of the programme might not yet be active; such as graduation, grievance redressing and others to be identified during the data collection.

Although the UPSNP provides conditional and unconditional transfer for beneficiaries, the study gives emphasis to livelihoods and asset of households' so as to describe their welfare conditions such as food security condition and improvements in livelihoods after receiving transfers. The beneficiaries' perception towards the programme is also assessed to understand the beneficiaries' satisfaction level regarding the delivery of programme, and here the study is limited methodologically in assessing their perceptions and knowledge, as their perceptions alone won't suffice for the much needed concrete information on the programme.

## 1.7 Ethical Considerations

The research took into account of research ethics, as this is mandatory for any study which considers following the scientific approaches of doing a research and which deems not to have any kind of impact on what is being studied. First issue of concern here was ensuring and getting the consent of the participants of the study. For this, before conducting the study, the university's official letter was sent to concerned bodies so as to obtain permission. Another was, when approaching respondents and participants of the study, the purpose of the study was explained at the beginning. Cognizant to this, complete permission was then asked before gathering the required information from the respondents. In addition, respondents were assured that any information which they give would be kept confidential and that it was going to be used for the purposes of this study only and will not be disclosed to anyone. Plus, any information which they would give for strengthening this study and information which could be against of the current UPSNP implementation process, by any way would not bring any impact in their PSNP beneficiary title or on the entitlements they have from programme.

## 1.8 Organization of the Thesis

The thesis is organized into five chapters. The first chapter covers the introduction section of the study. The second chapter reviews literatures pertaining to the study's thematic focus. The second chapter covers conceptual, theoretical and empirical issues relating to the study. Besides, the conceptual framework of the study is presented in the second chapter of the study. The third chapter on the other hand presents description of the study area and detailed research methodology followed throughout the study. The fourth chapter presents results of the analysis and interpretations of results and the last chapter concludes and brings plausible recommendations for the betterment of the UPSNP in the study area.

# Chapter Two

# Literature Review

This chapter of the study reviews literatures which are highly important and having a great relation to the focus of the study. Accordingly, the chapter is classified into five parts. The first section discusses the conceptual issues related to livelihood, components of food security, urban poverty, development of urban productive safety net programme in Ethiopia, components of the programme, community perception towards the programme and challenges to implement the programme. The second section talks about the theoretical approaches related to the study. The third section presents empirical studies on the productive safety net programme and the fourth and fifth sections describe the research gap and conceptual framework of the study.

## 2.1 Conceptual Framework

### *2.1.1 Livelihood and Livelihood Capitals*

Living is based on the capabilities, assets (stores, resources, claims and access) and activities required for a livelihood: a sustainable livelihood that can cope with and recover from stress and shocks, maintain or enhance its capabilities and assets, and provide the next generation with sustainable livelihood opportunities; and contributes net benefits to other livelihoods at regional and global levels in the short and long term (Krantz, 2001).

A sustainable livelihood approach describes resources as capital for livelihoods. Livelihood results include increased income, increased well-being and reduced vulnerability, improved food security and more sustainable use of natural resources. When income is higher than expenditure, it is sustainable (Sati & Vangchhia, 2017).

A livelihood involves the property and activities that a livelihood needs. Living is sustainable if it is able to cope with and rebound from shocks and stresses and preserve or improve its resources now and in the future (Woller, 2011). According to sustainable livelihood approach there are five major livelihood capitals Such as human capital, social capital, natural Capital, physical and financial capital.

Human capital: it encompass knowledge expertise, work skills and the physical state of good health which, when combined, helps people to engage with different strategies and achieve their own livelihood goals (UNDP, 2017). In addition to intangible character traits and health status, refer to the knowledge and capabilities of livelihoods available to individuals that determine how effectively individuals apply their knowledge and capabilities to livelihood activities (Woller, 2011).

Social Capital: refers to the social resources on which people can depend while following their livelihood objectives (in the present study, this specifically refers to local social capital, namely networks, organizations, local authorities, local officials and the broader population receiving program support) (UNDP, 2017). Social capital is created by the relationships of the household in a social network, and the values of confidence, reciprocity, and sharing of resources in those relations. It can be activated by households for social or social support or by communities to facilitate organization and collective action (Woller, 2011).

Natural Capital: is the term used to refer to natural resource stocks (soil, water, air, genetic resources, etc.) that can be used as inputs to create additional benefits such as food chains, soil or coastal erosion protection and other natural resources that can support livelihoods (UNDP, 2017). Physical and natural resource stocks that can be controlled by households and used to expand or enhance their livelihoods. Land, rivers, animals, ecosystems, and forestry are natural assets (Woller, 2011).

Physical capital: It relates to the basic infrastructure and inputs of production needed to support livelihoods (UNDP, 2017). The physical economic infrastructure, together with the productive assets of the household and other assets that enable the household to live among other issues, the physical economic infrastructure comprises highways, rail networks, communication centers, ports, etc. The productive assets of the household include land, machinery, tools, and animal drafting. Other physical assets in households include moving assets that can be converted to cash or exchanged for goods or services such as jewellery, furniture, electronics, appliances, or animals (Woller, 2011).

Financial capital: It applies to the financial resources that people use to achieve their survival goals (UNDP, 2017) . Financial assets are financial resources accessible to the family include deposits, loans, insurance, remittances, benefits, social welfare cash transfers and value-added property such as livestock and jewellery (Woller, 2011).

### *2.1.2 Food Security and Components of Food Security*

According to USAID (1992) as cited in woller, (2011), defined food security as 'when all people, at all times, have physical and economic access to sufficient, safe, and nutritious food to meet their dietary needs and food preferences for an active and healthy life" (Woller, 2011). Those who do not fulfill the conditions stated in the definition are considered as food insecure.

The Food and Agriculture Organization of the United Nations (FAO) defines food security as ensuring that all people at all times have both physical and economic access to the basic food that they need (FAO, 2003). At the World Food Summit in 1996, food security was defined as: "Food security exists when all people, at all times, have physical and economic access to sufficient, safe and nutritious food to meet their dietary needs, and food preferences for an active and healthy life" (FAO, UNICEF, WFP, et al, 2009). Food security has four sub-components: food availability, food access, food utilization and stability.

**Food availability**: refers to adequate quantities of appropriate, required types of domestic food, foreign imports, humanitarian aid programmes or food stocks are available to individuals consistently or within their reach so availability refers to the physical existence of food (Woller, 2011).

**Food access**: refers to individuals have adequate assets or incomes to produce, buy or purchase goods adequate foods needed to maintain adequate diet/nutrition level (Woller, 2011).

**Food utilization**: refers to the actual food consumed by individuals, how it is processed, prepared and consumed; and what nutritional benefits it receives from consumption (Woller, 2011).

**Food stability**: Food stability addresses the stability and sustainability of the other three dimensions over time. People cannot be considered food secure until they feel so and they do not feel food secure until there is stability of availability, accessibility and proper utilization condition. It refers to the ability to access and utilize appropriate levels of nutritious food over time (Woller, 2011).

Periodic insufficient access to food represents food insecurity. Food insecurity can be chronic or transitory depending on the duration of occurrence. Chronic food insecurity is a long-term or persistent failure to meet minimum requirements for food consumption, while transitory food insecurity is a short-term or temporary food deficit.

Ethiopia has recorded an overall reduction in rates of deprivation and food insecurity over the past 10 years. Poverty and food insecurity, however, remain a major challenge. For a healthy and active life, over 30 percent of the population is below the food poverty line, unable to afford the minimum caloric intake. Chronic malnutrition is severe, with 44% of children under the age of five stunted and 10% acute malnutrition affected (CSA and WFP, 2014).

In this research, food security focuses on the beneficiaries households 'food access status. In the scope of the research, food access refers to access at all times by beneficiary households to sufficient and appropriate food for an active and healthy life by means of income to buy or own produce. Food insecurity means households' inability to buy adequate and suitable food.

### *2.1.3 Urban Poverty*

According to UN- HABITAT (2006) one billion people – one-third of the urban population in the world is currently living in slums. Hundreds of millions of people in cities around the globe are living in desperate poverty without adequate shelter, clean water, and basic sanitation. Overcrowding and environmental degradation make urban poor particularly vulnerable to disease spread (Fernandez, 2007).

In comparison to rural poverty, urban poverty is complex and multidimensional, going beyond income or consumption deficiencies, where its several dimensions contribute to the insecurity of the poor due to inadequate access to land and housing, physical infrastructure and services, sources of economic and livelihood, health and education facilities, social security networks, and voice and empowerment. Urbanization was followed by poverty of slums and shelter, informality, deprivation of living conditions and growing threats due to climate change and urban exclusion (Bank, 2014).

In Ethiopia, urban poverty levels are quite large, particularly in the big cities. The differential in urban-rural poverty rates is low compared to other countries. The total number of heads of national poverty in 2011 was 29.6% (30.4% in rural Ethiopia and 25.7% in urban areas). Poverty rates were as high as 28.1% and 28.3% respectively in Addis Abeba and Dire Dawa (MoUDH, 2015).

As mentioned in MoUDH (2015) using the Survey of Household Income, Consumption and Expenditure (HICES) and Welfare Monitoring Survey (2010/11), the groups deemed to be urban poor in Ethiopia are:

The urban destitute: comprise homeless people, beggars and an infant on the streets. This demographic is the most influential portion of urban poverty, with 2.7% of the poorest urban household population.

The disabled and elderly with limited family support: This group includes the disabled and elderly persons who are unable to function and who are not employed for their homes. It is composed of 6.6% of urban poor.

Families who need more work: This category includes the large group of urban poor people in Ethiopia with little employment or low-quality jobs. Their status varies from homelessness to temporary work (marginal self-employment and low-wage work). This group of people makes up 41.7 percent of the country's urban population.

Families in marginal self-employment: This means household members involved in self-employment practices that do not make a great deal of income. The practices were small-scale business. This group includes 23.8 million of urban poor.

Families in low-wage employment: It covers families in low-wage jobs where people have income employment and are fully employed but do not receive enough to meet their household's needs. Employment is in services, construction, manufacturing, etc. About 24.6 million of Ethiopia's urban poor were listed as members of this category.

### *2.1.4 Urban Productive Safety Net Programme (UPSNP)*

#### Development of UPSNP in Ethiopia

Safety net programme is one component of social protection. According to Ministry of Labor and Social Affairs (2014), Social protection is part of the framework of social policy aimed at reducing poverty social and economic risks for people, vulnerability and exclusion by taking action through formal and informal processes to ensure inclusive and equitable development for all. This focuses on promoting productive safety net, promoting and strengthening jobs and wellbeing, promoting social security, ensuring equal access to basic social services, and providing legal protection and support for those vulnerable to violence and abuse.

Ethiopia's Productive Safety Net Programme (PSNP) is a large national social safety net (SSN) programme that not only addresses chronic food insecurity among the poor in Ethiopia, but also shocks in the short term, mainly droughts. In cooperation with international organizations, aid donors and civil society, the Government of Ethiopia (GoE) decided to complement the current reactive emergency food aid programme with a long-term solution to reduce food insecurity risk, called the National Food Security programme. A core element of the wider plan is the Productive Safety Nets Plan (PSNP)(World Bank, 2013).

The Productive Safety Net Programme (PSNP) has been operating in Ethiopia since 2005 in the rural parts of the country. The Ethiopian government extended the Productive Safety Net programme in to urban areas to alleviate food insecurity since 2016. Based on these experiences, the MoUDH has led the design of a systematic productive urban safety net and livelihood support intervention which will be implemented through a 10-year program framework. The long-term programme framework has an objective of reaching 4.7 million poor in 972 urban areas by implementing productive and predictable urban safety nets and complimentary livelihood interventions. The first phase supported by the UPSNP runs from 2016/17 to 2020/21 in 11 cities (Addis Ababa, Adama, Dessie, Mekele, Hawassa, Dire Dawa, Harari, Gambella, Asosa, Jigjiga and Asayita) and will focus on putting in place basic safety net building blocks, including productive and predictable transfers through public work, livelihood interventions, and capacity building. Given the large size of Addis Ababa and the relatively high poverty rates it records, about three-quarters of the beneficiaries will be from Addis Ababa (MoUDH, 2016).

## Components of UPSNP

To provide income support and increase employability UPSNP adopted a three-phase integrated model or pathway. According to the MoUDH (2016), in the first phase, clients will receive transfers (conditional on meeting their co-responsibilities) followed by life skills training and guidance on the employment pathways, namely self-employment and wage employment. In the second phase, client's s will continue to receive conditional transfers, training and job-matching services to increase employability. In the third phase, clients will have the option to continue to receive a small amount of conditional transfers to supplement income derived from employment secured as a result of programme support or through other means (MoUDH, 2016).

The three components of UPSNP are Safety Net Support, Livelihood Services, and Institutional Strengthening, Project Management and Coordination.

(a) **Safety Net Support:** This element enables consistent, timely and efficient safety net delivery through conditional and unconditional safety net transfers.

**Conditional Cash Transfers:** -In households eligible for programme support, conditional transfers will target capable bodied persons. This group represents an estimated 84% of the total beneficiaries of the programme. Under this component families with low wage jobs, who need more work to meet end and marginal self-employment included. A combination fall these factors means that families do not earn any income or earn enough to meet their food needs. Conditional transfers would include PW participation, ranging from small infrastructure to who need more work to make ends meet development of urban greenery and environmental and other services (MoUDH, 2016).

**Unconditional Cash Transfers:-** will target people who are unable to perform work for various reasons (e.g., the chronically ill, the elderly, the disabled, and the urban destitute). The unconditional transfer beneficiaries will reach up to 16 percent of the total programme beneficiaries (MoUDH, 2016).

There are two types of unconditional cash transfer beneficiaries.

**Permanent Unconditional Transfer Beneficiaries:** these are characterized as households that have no healthy and working age individuals able to participate in public works. All these features point to the fact the household is labor constrained and cannot participate in public works (MoUDH, 2016).

**Temporary Unconditional Transfer Beneficiaries:** These are defined as households who have lost their ability to engage in public works on a temporary basis and are excluded from public works for one or more of the following reasons Pregnant, lactating women with children under the age of one year, involuntary and unfit to work (MoUDH, 2016).

(b) **Livelihood Services:** According to PIM (2016), livelihood service aspect will help programmes aimed at encouraging programme graduation and supporting the transition out of poverty. The target groups for these measures are people in households receiving conditional transfers who want more and higher-paid work and a few recipients with business skills who engage directly in livelihood activities. There are two steps in supporting livelihoods counselling and life skill development and financial support and training for the development of livelihoods.

**Counselling and Life Skill Development**:- The first step of supporting livelihoods will focus on improving financial literacy and soft skills that will be useful across a variety of livelihood choices; evaluating beneficiaries 'technical skills; and providing individuals with knowledge about entrepreneurship and wage opportunities at their place (MoUDH, 2016).

**Financial Support and Training for the Development of Livelihoods:-** In the second phase of support for livelihoods, individuals receiving guidance in the first phase will choose whether to receive support to increase their self-employment income (either by starting a business or by increasing the profitability of an existing business) or wage employment (either by gaining access to wages) (MoUDH, 2016).

(c) **Institutional Strengthening and Programme Management:** This component will support the development and enhancement of programme systems for targeting, monitoring and evaluation and MIS, payments, and citizens' engagement (CE). It will also finance capacity building (human resource, training, administrative, and physical capacity) and strengthening programme management (coordination, Financial Management (FM), procurement, and safeguards) (MoUDH, 2016).

## Contributions of UPSNP

The UPSNP has interventions that meet the varied needs of the urban poor and vulnerable. UPSNP supports the development of beneficiaries capitals in a number of ways. To summarize, it contributes to financial capital by providing cash payments for days worked; and grants as required, to human capital by promoting functional literacy classes among adults and helping parents send their children to school instead of work, to social capital by building clients' confidence to engage in community affairs and strengthen their social the network and to natural/physical capital by applying watershed management approach adopted by the programme contributes to the development of natural resources and also contribute to the development objectives of the government clean, green and safer cities (MoUDH, 2016). In describing the specific role of the programme, it attempts to improve the food security and income status of households as well as the living environment of communities in order to address the urban poor's living insecurity.

## Community Perceptions towards Productive Safety Net Programme

The attitude of the community towards the programme ranges from targeting both on beneficiaries and non-beneficiaries until graduation. The behavior of PSNP beneficiaries about graduation is somewhat unclear. The concerns, for instance, applied to their desire to transfer from the Programme and continue or remain eligible for as long as possible. Questions like the PSNP generated 'self-confidence' or developed a mentality of 'dependency differently perceived by beneficiaries and non-beneficiaries. A more common attitude is that beneficiaries agree they are in fact prepared to graduate, but they do not feel ready and want more time and additional support until they exit the programme." When we compare PSNP beneficiary and non-beneficiary households there is a change for non-beneficiaries because beneficiaries are highly dependent on help – they are expecting help – and they always have fear, they don't want to work hard on their farms, they are selling and renting their land instead of working on it, they don't want to graduate from PSNP, whereas non-beneficiaries don't expect anything from the government so they are working day and night on their land (Devereux et al, 2014).

## Challenges for Implementing Productive Safety Net Programme

According to Wondim, (2018) PSNP has both positive and negative effects on the cultural, economic and environmental growth of the beneficiaries. The government should therefore consider social, financial, environmental and available resources prior to implementation. The bodies concerned should therefore consider the impact of the PSNP and family support on the wellbeing of the beneficiaries and should depend on information from the panel data (Wondim, 2018).

Capacity, graduation and dependence philosophies, and timeliness of transfers and donor support were the factors that hindered the programme. The other problem or obstacle facing programme implementation was insufficient financial resources. As a result, the programme allowed a small number of beneficiaries to participate. The programmes problems are geographical location, administrative (selection process used for qualifying households) and removal of the vulnerable with the inclusion of rich, low social linkages and lack of active community participation in decision-making (Wondim, 2018).

The challenges facing the implementation of PSNP were the inclusion and exclusion of beneficiaries, weak management and restriction of beneficiaries' awareness official contact issues, lack of manpower in remote areas, lack of control and assessment of locally built infrastructure for sustainability (Wondim, 2018).

## 2.2 Theoretical Framework

This section of the study presents theoretical underpinnings for this study which include conceptual developments and theories that are pertinent to this study.

### *2.2.1 The Basic Need Approach*

In 1976, the International Labor Organization (ILO), with the goal of integrating non-economic aspects of growth has proposed a new development model, the basic needs approach. The main causes of the policy shift were the problems of inequality, unemployment and underemployment, reported in periods of rising economic growth. The advocates of basic needs approached development as a process aimed at ensuring that their basic needs were met by all people. Food is a basic need probably the most basic need of all .This approach focuses specifically on whether people eat enough food and has helped to shift the study from the macro level to the micro level. Food is regarded as a priority (and possibly the only) food security item (Burchi & Muro, 2012).

### *2.2.2 The Entitlement Approach*

The entitlement approach to poverty and starvation relies on people's ability to order food through the legal means present in society, including the use of development resources, trade opportunities, state entitlements and other forms of food procurement. A human starves either because he is not able to order enough food, or because he is not using this ability to avoid starvation. The entitlement approach emphasizes on the entitlements of each individual to packages of goods and food, and recognizes deprivation as a consequence of inability to be entitled to a package of sufficient food. The entitlement method emphasizes on poverty, which must be differentiated from famine mortality, as many of the starvation deaths — in some instances most of them — are triggered by epidemics that have their own trends(Sen, 1982).

### *2.2.3 The Human Rights Approach*

Extreme Poverty is the biggest human rights issue in the

world. In line with the UN Universal Declaration of Human Rights, Finland's human rights-based development policy begins with the idea that all human beings are born free and equal in status and rights. Development based on human rights includes civil and political rights and freedoms as well as economic, social and cultural rights. Particular attention will be given to the rights and equal opportunities of vulnerable people and those who are socially excluded and discriminated (Sepúlveda & Nyst, 2012).

As stated in Sepulveda and Nyst (2012), the relationship between extreme poverty and the enjoyment of human rights, each are a cause and consequence of the other which makes poverty a major human rights issue. Justice and non-discrimination, including availability, adaptability, and acceptability, adequacy and gender context inclusion), involvement, transparency and accountability for the development, implementation, monitoring and evaluation of social protection programs are principles of human right approach.

Human right approach, contribute to ending extreme poverty. In addition, an approach to human rights empowers those living in poverty and adds legitimacy as it refers to a set of norms and values universally accepted. Human rights can provide practical guidance in designing, implementing, assessing and monitoring efforts to reduce poverty. Because human rights seek to empower the poor, efforts to alleviate poverty fundamentally shift from a charity or needs-based approach to rights and towards a concentration on rights and entitlements. As a consequence, the approach to human rights has the potential to improve the efficiency of efforts to reduce poverty and ensure that progress is equal and sustainable (Sepúlveda & Nyst, 2012).

### *2.2.4 The Empowerment Approach*

Empowerment approach can be implemented to improve the well-being of life at individual, organizational and even community levels to a better state. Approach to empowerment, discuss the issues of poverty, education, women, people with disabilities, single mothers, youth, governance, organizations and so on, is an innovative approach to solving challenges by encouraging individuals or groups to take effective action through the capacity and potential created (Ani, 2017).

According Ani, (2017) the path to empowerment is addressed and directly linked to community members 'involvement in the development process. This is because participation is the main objective and purpose of the social mobilization process. In short, empowerment is a mechanism through which individuals and groups contribute their knowledge and ability to understand and articulate issues and needs that are then transformed into practice through active participation.

This approach is widely recognized as a practical approach that can improve capacity and ability to achieve a better level of community life. In the development, community empowerment happens as they demonstrate the ability to identify problems, gain resources, build skills and experience, adopt, lead and organize all members of the community to participate actively in each mutually beneficial project (Ani, 2017).

### *2.2.5 The Sustainable Livelihood Framework*

The Brundtland Commission on Environment and Development first introduced the idea of sustainable livelihoods as a way to link socio-economic and ecological concerns into a coherent, policy-relevant framework. The 1992 United Nations Conference on Environment and

Development (UNCED) extended the definition, particularly in the context of Agenda 21 (Krantz, 2001). Since the 1990s, sustainable livelihood theory has influenced the practice of development organizations. UNDP has been one of the early participants and contributors to this conceptual framework. The system for livelihoods provides the skills, resources (both physical and social) and strategies that individuals and communities will use to survive. The resilience aspect ensures that these individuals or groups can cope with and resolve periods of pressure and/or crisis and are able to maintain or even develop current and future skills and resources (UNDP, 2017).

According to UNDP (2017) applying sustainable livelihood approach requires the following aspects an understanding of vulnerability in a given context, a strategy to protect livelihoods, an analysis of different types of capital (human capital, social capital, natural capital, physical capital and financial capital.)

According to DFID (1999) as citied in (Krantz, 2001) the sustainable livelihood framework is not intended to be an exact model of reality, but to provide an analytical structure to facilitate a broad and systematic understanding of the various factors that constrain or enhance livelihood opportunities, and to show how they relate to each other. It should further be noted that the framework as such does not lay down any explicit definition of what exactly constitutes poverty, which is context-specific and therefore must be investigated on a case-by-case basis with different groups.

SL Approach creates a more holistic view of what resources are important to the poor, including not only physical and natural resources, but also their social and human capital. The approach also promotes an understanding of the underlying causes of poverty by reflecting on the variety of factors at various levels that directly or indirectly decide or limit the access of poor people to different kinds of resources/ assets and thus their livelihoods (Krantz, 2001).

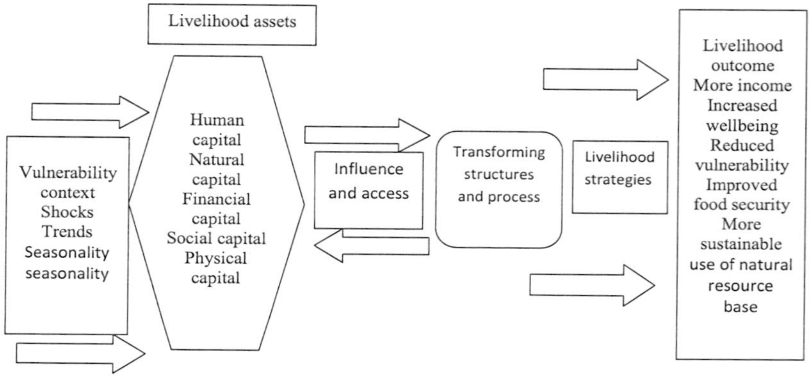


*Figure 2.1: Sustainable Livelihoods Framework. Graph from DFID (1999)*

## 2.3 Empirical Review

There have been many studies on contribution of social safety net (SSN) programme in various parts of the world. For instance studies had been carried out in Bangladesh (2018), Social Safety Nets Programmes: contribution to socio economic resilience of vulnerable group. The result shows that the programme has a positive impact on the basic needs like food, cloth, medicine accessibility of the beneficiaries which make them economically resilient, has positive impact on daily food intake pattern due to this programme vulnerable communities are able to meet their basic need and also it has positive impacts on the community in aspects of poverty to solvency.

There are a number of researches conducted in Ethiopia related to Productive Safety Net Programme (PSNP). Diriba (2017) had tried to assess the contribution of Productive Safety Net Programme for food security of the rural households.

The result indicated that PSNP was helping beneficiaries for consumption smoothing, asset accumulation, and development of the local community.

Desta (2017) studied the practice and challenges of PSNP in SNNPR in Gamo highlands. As the study result shows that PSNP improved asset building and child education of beneficiaries and also it increased asset building to community through food for work scheme.

Gelebo (2010) studied the contribution of the Productive Safety Net Programme (PSNP) to household asset building in selected kebeles of konso special woreda. The result shows that PSNP has been less successful in rebuilding a strong asset base that could enable the graduation of many poor households out of food insecurity. The study has found that low rate and delay of payments, overlap of PSNP-public works programme with local farming season, absence of the integration of PSNP with other food security programme interventions, transfer of resources that does not meet beneficiary preferences, poverty and droughts were impediments that constrained the potential of the programme.

## 2.4 Research Gap

As mentioned above, most studies reviewed especially those outside of Ethiopia focused on social safety nets in urban areas, whereas those studies conducted in Ethiopian majorly focused on the rural settings of the PSNP. Most researchers worked on the contribution of the safety net to food security, income generation, poverty alleviation, asset ownership, and household resilience. Since the urban safety net programme is newly introduced in Ethiopia, limited studies are conducted on the area. Therefore, studying the beneficiary households' food access and their livelihood improvement after joining the programme provides information about their status and acts as baseline information for determining the effect of the programme in the future. It is also necessary to allow programme implementers to understand the actual situation of the beneficiaries and to take appropriate measures to implement the programme effectively. In this situation, deprivation and vulnerability of the urban poor can be better alleviated. This research thus aims to fill this gap by brining baseline information that can assist to respond to the commitment of the UPSNP in improving the livelihoods of beneficiary households specifically in Dire Dawa City Administration.

## 2.5 Conceptual Framework of the Study

The study used sustainable livelihood frame work of Department for International Development (DFID) as its conceptual framework. SLF provides a useful analytical basis for understanding urban poverty and the situation of people living in urban settlements in poverty, and is an effective tool for evaluating the effects of legislation on their living condition.

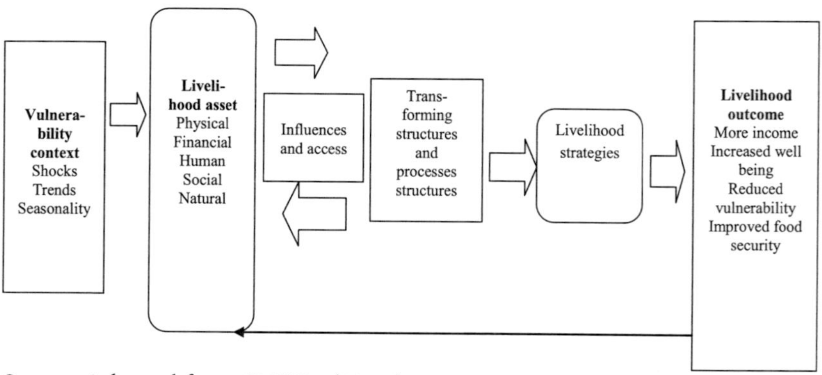


*Source:* Adapted from DFID, (19 99).

*Figure 2.2: Conceptual Framework of the Study*

As shown in Figure 2.2, the framework includes the vulnerability context, assets, transforming structures and processes, livelihood strategies, livelihood outcomes. The arrows in the figure indicate the influence of each other. Depending on the model, the vulnerability context (shocks, trends and seasonality) affects the people's asset. The transforming systems and processes decide people's access to various types of assets and the type of livelihood strategy used to develop livelihoods.

In a number of ways, the Urban Productive Safety Net Programme facilitates the growth of beneficiaries assets. The system increases the beneficiaries social asset (social networks), financial assets (income and savings), human assets (food safety, skills and work habits), natural assets (environmental protection) and physical assets (household assets). This offers a safe and alternative means of living for families in addition to other livelihoods (wage labor, small business and low-wage jobs). The programme would allow them to engage with better livelihood strategies with better results by improving their asset.

# Chapter Three

# Research Methodology

This study was intended to assess the contribution of Urban Productive Safety Net Programme to households' livelihood improvement in Dire Dawa City Administration. In this regard, this section of the research deals with a short introduction about the study area and the methodological plans of the research. Accordingly, this part of the study contains the description of the study area, research design, sampling technique, sample size, source and type of data, data collection tools and methods, and data analysis methods.

## 3.1 Description of the Study Area

Proclamation No. 416/2004 provides Dire Dawa Administration a legal status that enables it to become a chartered city. The residents have, therefore, a legal foundation that enables them exercise self-administration and can determine the organizational structures and operations of the city. As per this proclamation, Dire Dawa Administration has the mandate to design, and carryout development undertakings that enables it to address its socio economic problems. Dire Dawa Administration has two tiers of government structure: administration & Kebele levels (DDAC, 2014).

### Location

Dire Dawa City is located between 90 27' N and 9049' N latitude and 41038'E and 42019'E longitude. East Hararge

Administrative Zone of Oromiya Regional State borders it in the south and southeast and Shinele Zone of Somali Regional State in the north, east and west. Dire Dawa city is accessible by airplane, train, and cars, and it is about 515kms away from Addis Ababa and 311kms to the west of the port of Djibouti. It has a total land area of 128,802 ha, of which 97.73% covers the rural area and the remaining 2.27% the urban area (DDAC, 2014).

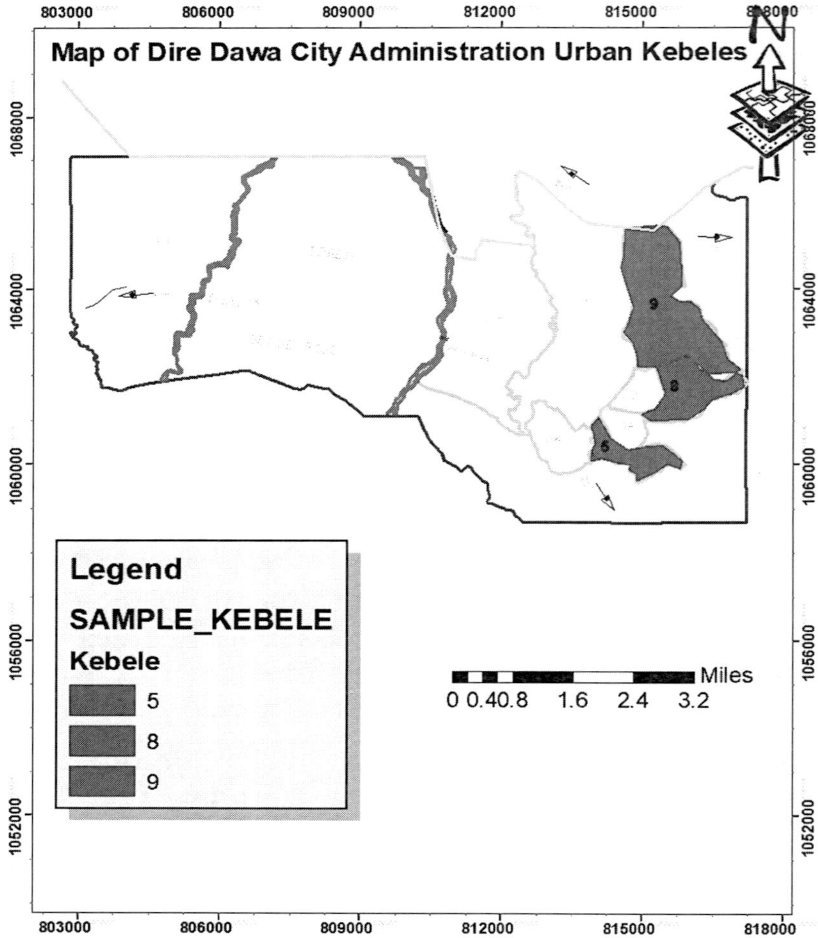


*Source:* Dire Dawa City Administration Land Management Bureau, (2020)

***Figure 3.1: Map of Dire Dawa City Administration by Sample***

## Demography

According to United Nations population projection report the current population of Dire Dawa Administration in 2019 is 391,000 a 4.27 % increase from 2018 (United Nations, 2019).

## Socio Economic Condition

Dire Dawa can be regarded as the most ethnically and religiously diversified city, where all live in harmony. In this regard, it is the second city administration next to the capital city of Ethiopia; Addis Ababa. The predominant religions in the area are Islam and Christianity.

Dire Dawa's strategic geographic location between Addis Ababa and the port of Djibouti has accorded it various economic and commercial advantages. It serves as transit and terminal for import and export of commodities and services. Import export trade thus characterizes the town's economic structure. Trade and industry are the predominant sectors of Dire Dawa's economy (DDAC, 2014).

Out of a total nine urban Kebeles, the study has chosen three Kebeles namely; 05, 08 and 09 Kebeles as the study site. Beneficiary households from the programme are present in these selected Kebeles.

## 3.2 Research Methodology

This section of the study presents the research design, data source, sampling techniques and sample size determination, data collection methods and data analysis methods.

### *3.2.1 Research Design*

This study employed descriptive research design using mixed approach of both qualitative and quantitative approaches in order to develop a comprehensive analysis of the phenomenon study. In line to this, based on the objectives of the study, from the different types of survey research methodologies, cross sectional research design was used in this study so as to gather information from a sample at one point in time.

## Quantitative approach

For quantitative approach survey research method was used as this method allows collecting a breadth of data from large samples and generalizing to the larger population from which the samples were drawn from. To gather information for the quantitative data, questionnaire was used as a survey tool.

## Qualitative approach

In addition to the quantitative approach, qualitative approach was also used with the aim of getting deep understanding about the programme and its contribution to improve households' livelihoods. In this regards, Key Informant Interview (KII) and Focus Group Discussion (FGD) were used as data collection tools. The qualitative approach was deemed to bring significant and additional information to supplement and triangulate the information to be gathered for the quantitative survey. Besides, the use of qualitative approach was expected to have significant addition by fetching information which would not have been possible to gather through the quantitative survey. That is, the qualitative one was employed with the belief that it would broaden the scope of the quantitative approach and as a supplement for triangulation purposes.

### *3.2.2 Data Source*

The study used both primary and secondary sources of data to undertake this research. The primary data were collected from respondents through questionnaire; Key Informant

Interviews and Focus Group Discussion so as to get first-hand information. In addition to this, secondary data were gathered and used in the study. The secondary information were collected from published and unpublished documents of the programme, researches, articles, and reports related to the study from different institutions including Ministry of Agriculture, Urban Food Security and Job Creation Offices, Kebele level UPSNP implementation offices and international donor organizations of the programme.

### *3.2.3 Sampling Techniques and Sample Size Determination*

**Sampling Technique**

Both probability and non-probability sampling technique were used to undertake the selection of respondents at different stages of the selection. First by using non-probability sampling three Kebeles from nine urban Kebeles were purposively selected as they had started implementation of the programme early which makes it pertinent for this study to assess the contribution of the programme to households' livelihood improvement thoroughly. Furthermore, probability sampling was employed to choose beneficiaries so as to give beneficiaries equal chance of being selected from the selected Kebeles. Accordingly, beneficiary households were chosen randomly to conduct the survey from a listing gathered from Kebele level Offices who are in charge of implementing UPSNP in Dire Dawa City.

**Sample Size Determination**

Sample size estimation formula of Yamane (1967) was used to determine the sample size of the study. The required sample sizes were determined at 95 percent confidence level and with 0.05 margin of error. The reason for using the formula is because the formula is valid for survey researches which are having known population size (Yamane 1967).

$$n = \frac{N}{1+Ne^2}, \text{ (Yamane1967)}$$

n = sample size N = the size of the population e = the margin of error, 5%

Applying this formula $n = \frac{3898}{1+3898(0.05)2} = 363$

Total sample sizes of 363 beneficiary households from the three Kebeles were the target sample population for the study.

To select beneficiaries from the selected Kebeles, quota sampling of (public work 84% and direct support 16%) was set. This is set basing on the information which revealed that 84% of the beneficiaries are Public Work beneficiaries and the remaining 16% are direct support beneficiaries as stated in a report from the City Administration. Accordingly, using Probability Proportional to Size (PPS) a total of 58 direct support beneficiaries and 305 conditional beneficiary households (Public work beneficiaries) had participated in the survey.

In line to this, the PPS was again used to allocate the number of participants of the study among the three selected Kebeles. Accordingly, the total households in each Kebele is multiplied by the calculated sample size (363) and divided by the number of total households in selected Kebeles so as to get the weights and samples per each Kebele.

Sample size in each Kebele

$$= \frac{\text{total HH in each Kebele} \times \text{calculated sample size (363)}}{\text{Number of total HH in selected Kebeles}}$$

Thus, from Kebele 05 (15 direct support beneficiaries and 80 conditional beneficiaries), from Kebele 08(20 direct beneficiaries and 106 conditional beneficiaries) and lastly, from Kebele 09 (23 direct beneficiaries and 119 conditional beneficiaries) were selected for survey.

**Table 3.1 Sample Size Allocation per Kebele and Beneficiary Type**

| *Study Kebele* | *Total households* | | | *Sample households* | | |
|---|---|---|---|---|---|---|
| | *No of beneficiary households* | | | *Sample beneficiary households* | | |
| | *PW (84%)* | *DS (16%)* | *Total HH* | *PW* | *DS* | *Total HH* |
| 05 | 700 | 322 | 1022 | 80 | 15 | 95 |
| 08 | 862 | 492 | 1354 | 106 | 20 | 126 |
| 09 | 1186 | 336 | 1522 | 119 | 23 | 142 |
| Total | 2748 | 1150 | 3898 | 305 | 58 | 363 |

### *3.2.4 Data Collection Methods*

Both quantitative and qualitative types of data were used in order to collect the much needed information about UPSNP and livelihoods from the respondents. To conduct the survey, the study used trained enumerators and for the actual data collection, the enumerators used translated version of the questionnaire for ease and reliable information gathering. The method involved for both types of data which are discussed in detail as follows.

#### Quantitative Data Collection Method

For collecting the data for the quantitative type, questionnaires were used. The questionnaires were used to gather information from the sample 363 beneficiary households. By using questionnaires; it was deemed that it will fetch information concerning households' demographic, socio-economic, livelihood status, households' food access and beneficiaries' perception towards the programme delivery and related information.

## Qualitative Data Collection Method

#### Key Informant Interview (KII)

Key Informant Interview was undertaken with different

knowledgeable individuals who know the issue related to Urban Productive Safety Net Programme in the city administration. The respondents for KII were selected purposefully based on their knowledge towards the programme. To mention few, interview was conducted with experts working in Urban Job Creation and Food Security Agency, Bureau of Labour and Social Affairs, and experts at Kebele level, and etc. They were interviewed so as to get information about UPSNP implementation especially on information related to households' livelihood related activities and implementation challenges of the programme.

**Focus Group Discussion (FGD)**

The study also used focus group discussions in order to obtain detailed information and in order to complement and triangulate information gathered through questionnaire and key informant interviews. The programmes role in building households asset and the values added on food access, plus beneficiaries' perception towards the programme and implementation challenges were discussed. Concomitantly, three focus group discussions were carried after purposively selecting participants and each group contained six participants each. Targeting committee member, appeals committee member, direct support beneficiary, public work beneficiary, public direct support beneficiary and an expert were included in each group.

### *3.2. 5 Data Analysis Methods*

**Quantitative Data Analysis**

Data collected by questionnaire from beneficiary households from each Kebele was edited, coded and entered a computer for analysis using Statistical Packages for Social Science (SPSS) software. The study used descriptive statistics for analyzing the quantitative data. Descriptive statistics such as frequency, percentages, cross tabulation; bar graphs and pie charts, means, chi-square test and others were used to interpret the results as needed.

### Qualitative Data Analysis

Data collected through key informant interview and focus group discussions were analyzed using thematic analysis. The analysis process followed different phases. First, the data were organized per type of beneficiary and transcription was done, and then were re-organized and coded. Then, the listed codes were categorized into themes. Once again, the themes were examined if they reflect and capture clearly and accurately the data collected. Finally, the themes and sub-themes established and the information that matched under each theme were written in a direct quote (through narration) or paraphrased as needed.

Chapter Four

# Results and Discussions

This chapter presents analysis and discussion of the results. The first section summarizes the general background of the sample households and the second section describes the perceptions of beneficiaries on UPSNP. The third section dealt about contributions of UPSNP to households' livelihood assets and food assess. The last part in this chapter presents challenges in the implementation of UPSNP. Overall, the sub-titles and report write-up followed the orders of the specific objectives of the study so as to ensure that each is addressed properly.

## 4.1. General Background of Respondents

This section presents background characteristics of the study participants which were about 363.These characteristics include sex, age, religion, educational status, marital status, and type of programme beneficiary. These are presented as follows;

**Table 4.1 Socio Demographic Characteristics of Respondents**

| | *Attributes* | *Frequencies* | *Percentage (%)* |
|---|---|---|---|
| Sex of the household head | Male | 160 | 44.1 |
| | Female | 203 | 55.95 |
| | Total | 363 | 100 |
| Age of the household head | 21-40 | 152 | 41.9 |
| | 41-60 | 171 | 47.1 |
| | Above 60 | 40 | 11 |
| | Total | 363 | 100 |

*(Contd...)*

| | | | |
|---|---|---|---|
| Religion of the respondent | Orthodox | 132 | 36.4 |
| | Muslim | 201 | 55.4 |
| | Protestant | 26 | 7.2 |
| | Catholic | 4 | 1.1 |
| | Total | 363 | 100 |
| Marital status of respondent | Married | 186 | 51.2 |
| | Single | 50 | 13.8 |
| | Divorced | 62 | 17.1 |
| | Widowed | 65 | 17.9 |
| | Total | 363 | 100 |
| Type of beneficiary | Public work | 305 | 84 |
| | Direct support | 58 | 16 |
| | Total | 363 | 100 |

*Source:* Own Field Survey, (2020)

From the total sample households, female headed households covered were about 203(55.95%) and the remaining 160(44.1%) were male headed households. The findings in this study showed that, the majority beneficiaries are female headed households, which could perhaps is related to the direct support given to women having larger number of household members. Besides this, female headed households are mostly vulnerable and affected by food insecurity than male-headed households. Similar to this finding, Gezimu (2012) found that food insecurity was is more prevalent among female headed household in Addis Ababa (Gezimu, 2012). Badassa (2018), also indicated that female headed households had high probability to participate in the food security programmes than their male counterparts due to their vulnerability (Badassa Wolteji Chala, 2018).

From the total respondents, 171(47.1%) were in the age range between 41 - 60 years age group, followed by 152(41.9%) in the age group of 21-40 years and 40(11%) aged above 60 years. 305(84%) of the sample households are conditional beneficiaries who are engaged in physical labor work in the Urban productive Safety Net Programme (UPSNP) and the remaining 58(16%) are direct support beneficiaries. Majority

351(96.7%) of the respondents' are beneficiary for three years in UPSNP in the study area. For conditional beneficiaries transfers are made evenly throughout the year on monthly basis after completing public works whereas unconditional transfers beneficiaries are persons that for various reasons are unable to work (chronically ill, the elderly and people with disabilities, urban destitute female headed households with large household size and etc) as stated in programme implementation manual. It was also found that most of the respondents who are under productive age group (above 18 years) majorly participate in public work activities of the programme. From the total of participants in this study, 186(51.2%) are married, 50(13.8%) were single, 62(17.1%) were divorced and 65(17.9%) were widowed Majority of participants were Muslims 201(55.4%), 132(36.4%) were Orthodox, 26(7.2%) were Protestant and 4(1.1%) were Catholics.

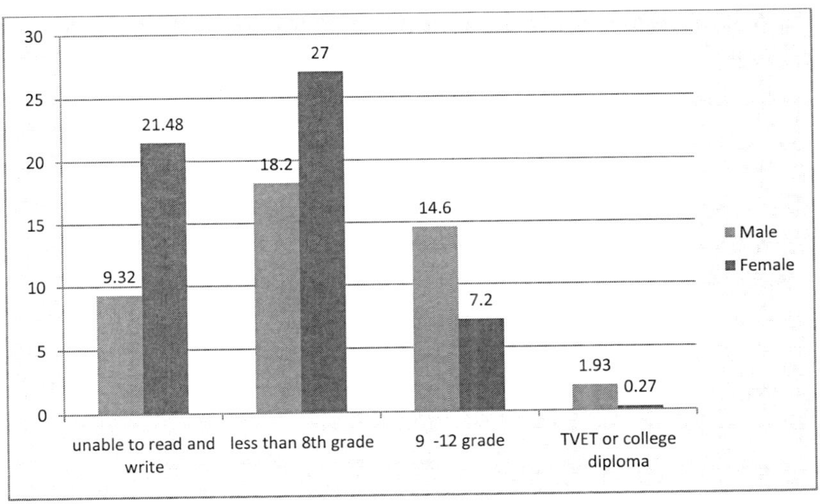


*Source:* Own Computation, (2020)

***Figure 4.1: Educational Levels of the Household Head.***

respondents, 30.8% participants were unable to read and write, among those that attended formal education 45.2%

have completed primary education, 21.8% completed secondary education and 2.2% had college diploma. However, low literacy level (who only completed primary and secondary education) accounts most of the study population. This low level of educational attainment could hamper their ability and competitiveness in getting better jobs in the market as education improves the knowledge and skills which are essential to get higher paying jobs and limits households from improving their livelihoods. Further assessment on educational data shows that females' educational attainment level was comparably lower than their male counterparts. According to Degefa (2008), individuals with low educations have limited chances of getting employment in better jobs due to high competition of job market. Degefa also added that low educational level hinders household from participating in high paying jobs; as a result of this, they engage in low paying jobs which barely sustain their livelihoods. These factors generally make households to remain poor and lead a life under the vicious circle of poverty.

**Table 4.2 Marital Status and Sex of Households by Type of Beneficiary**

| *Beneficiary Type* | *Marital Status* | *Sex of the HH* | | *Total* |
|---|---|---|---|---|
| | | *Male* | *Female* | |
| Public Work | Married | 110 | 56 | 166 |
| | Single | 18 | 28 | 46 |
| | Divorced | 9 | 45 | 54 |
| | Widowed | 3 | 36 | 39 |
| | Total | 140 | 165 | 305 |
| Direct Support | Married | 14 | 6 | 20 |
| | Single | 2 | 2 | 4 |
| | Divorced | 0 | 8 | 8 |
| | Widowed | 4 | 22 | 26 |
| | Total | 20 | 38 | 58 |

*Source:* Own Field Survey, (2020)

The survey result in Table 4.2 above, large proportions of both male and female headed public work beneficiaries were married. Out of 38 female headed direct support beneficiaries, majority 22 households were widowed and 8 were divorced. The survey shows large proportions of female headed direct support beneficiaries were widowed. This result aligns greatly with the selection criteria of direct support beneficiaries which includes female headed households with higher number of members.

**Table 4.3 No of Family Members in the Household**

| *Sex of the HH head* | *Beneficiary type* | *Household size* | |
|---|---|---|---|
| | | *Less than three* | *Four and more than four* |
| Male | Public Work | 85 | 56 |
| | Direct Support | 18 | 1 |
| | Total | 103 | 57 |
| Female | Public Work | 109 | 55 |
| | Direct Support | 35 | 4 |
| | Total | 144 | 59 |

*Source:* Own Field Survey, (2020)

As shown in the above table the majority of both public work and direct support beneficiaries are female headed households have less than 4 household sizes. The mean household size of the respondents had 1.32 and by beneficiary, mean household size of public work beneficiaries is 1.36 and direct support beneficiaries is 1.09.

Different researches express a household who have large family size has a higher probability of falling into poverty. Other studies findings show that as the family size of the household increases, the incidence of poverty also increases (Hagos, 2014) and those households with large family sizes, large dependents, and young heads were food insecure (Eneyew, 2012). According to CSA (2016), report the average household size in Ethiopia is 4.6 persons. Urban households are slightly smaller than rural households 3.5 persons versus 4.9 persons (CSA, 2016).

This study result shows from the total 305 public work respondents' 260 have one economically active member in their household and the remaining 45 respondents have two economically active members. From the total 58 direct support beneficiaries 26 respondents have one economically active member in their household and the remaining 32 respondents do not have any economically active member in their household. The direct support beneficiaries targeting has some flawed issues as about 44.8% have economically active member which disqualifies them being a direct beneficiary.

**Table 4.4 Health status of the Household Member**

| *Beneficiary Type* | *Health Problem (%)* | *No Health Problem (%)* | *Total (%)* |
|---|---|---|---|
| Public Work | 84(27.5) | 221(72.5%) | 305(100) |
| Direct Support | 32(55.2%) | 26(44.8%) | 58(100) |
| Total | 116 | 247 | 363 |

*Source:* Own Field Survey, (2020)

As the above Table 4.4 result shows, more than half of direct support beneficiary household members had serious health problems than public work beneficiaries. This finding also bring into line with the notion of direct support beneficiary selection categories is a household having serious health issues which deters from participating in any public labor participation which is conditional for transfers. Those having different health related problems in their family members are often forced to stay dormant economically and inactive or dependent and this perhaps with no doubts affects their livelihood status negatively.

## 4.2. Perceptions of Beneficiaries about UPSNP

The respondents' perception with regard to UPSNP was assessed in terms of targeting process of the beneficiaries, support appropriateness, timeliness of cash transfers and the general effect of the programme on beneficiaries' livelihoods. In the survey, assessment was also made on the satisfaction level of the respondents using scales ranging from very unsatisfied to very satisfied. In concomitant to these, findings from key informant interviews and the focus group discussions are also built-in with the household survey results.

### *4.2.1. Targeting*

Targeting is undertaken at household level in order to select the poor household who are eligible to be included in the programme. Beneficiaries are selected through community based targeting mechanism and also there is an appeal mechanism to avoid inclusion and exclusion errors as stated in Implementation Manual.

In so doing, respondents were inquired if they have the necessary information about the programme targeting. Majority 348(95.9%) of respondents stated that they received prior information about Urban Productive Safety Net Programme, regarding its targeting and procedures for being a beneficiary, although the remaining 15(4.1%) did not. Besides, 340 (93.7%) respondents said that the information they received is useful for understanding the targeting procedures of the programme. Overall, it can be noted that majority households were made aware about the programme and the targeting processes which is one of the prerequisites for the successful implementation of the programme (MoUDH, 2016).

**Table 4.5 Beneficiaries Satisfaction in Targeting**

| *Level of Satisfaction* | *Public Work* | *Direct support* | *Total* |
|---|---|---|---|
| Very Unsatisfied | 17 | 4 | 21 |
| Somehow Unsatisfied | 45 | 7 | 52 |
| Neutral | 10 | 8 | 18 |
| Somehow Satisfied | 195 | 31 | 226 |
| Very Satisfied | 38 | 8 | 46 |
| Total | 305 | 58 | 363 |

*Source:* Own Field Survey, (2020)

The survey result indicates the majority of both public work and direct support respondents are of the view that they are at least to some extent respondents satisfied on the targeting process of beneficiaries This satisfaction is deemed to be vital in this study as it can reveal if there are blemished and inconsistencies in selection of beneficiaries to the programme. That is, beneficiary selection could be susceptible arbitrariness, subjectivity and partiality if households who do not meet the requirements of the targeting are selected in later stages (false selection); i.e. better-off households selected as beneficiaries and poorest of the poor not being excluded from participation. Concomitantly, this study says otherwise, meaning, the targeting results above combined with the satisfaction of household's shows that the programme is in compliance with the implementation manual.

**The targeting of beneficiaries was described during FGDs as:**

> *The targeting of beneficiaries is undertaken by publically selected and trained community members to select the poorest of the poor among the households based on the criteria set in the implementation manual. Eligible households with able bodied adults are targeted for conditional transfer (public work). Those who are unable to work because of disability, illness, age... are targeted for unconditional transfers throughout the year. The identified poor are screened in front of community members for validation. Those who were missed in the selection process had been included in the screening process. An appeal created in the targeting process is due to quota targeting as all the poor who need aid are not targeted to benefit from the programme. Due to their unavailability during the selection process, some households missed the opportunity and were substituted by new households. Some individuals who are eligible for public work but selected for conditional transfers have appealed in the*

> *targeting process of beneficiaries. Lack of uniformity in targeting criteria application among targeting committees has brought exclusion of some poor households. (FGD, February 18, 2020, Dire Dawa)*

Other studies had mentioned the limitation of PSNPs is targeting process in the rural parts of Ethiopia. For instance a study in Bale Zone Saweyna Woreda PSNP coordinator has pointed out that there was a false inclusion and exclusion of beneficiaries where better off individuals were found to be wrongly included, particularly in pastoral areas and individuals affected worst by food insecurity were wrongly excluded (Welteji, et al 2017). According to Yitagesu (2014), targeting of beneficiaries was having some difficult decisions to make because of limited quota provided for the Woreda.

According to Urban Job Creation and Food Security Agency and Labour and Social Affair team leaders, as a pilot project the programme gives priority for the poorest of the poor based on the criteria stated in the manual for the proper selection of beneficiaries. Households with able bodied and economically active member are able to work but vulnerable and not able to meet their food needs are entitled for public work and those who have no healthy and working age individual to participate in public works are entitled for direct support. For this, trainings were given for targeting committees on how to conduct the selection and the criteria used for selection of beneficiaries. Furthermore, awareness can be created for the beneficiaries about the programme by using different communication hierarchies. So the programme tries to deliver the necessary information for the beneficiaries. Meetings are held regularly between public work beneficiaries and team leaders, Kebele coordinators and the agency. But direct support beneficiaries are not frequently called for meetings due to their conditions and thus there is a gap in awareness about the programme between these two beneficiaries of the programme. But, overall the results here settle to the ideal that most beneficiaries are satisfied with the programme's information delivery process and targeting.

### *4.2.2 Support Appropriateness*

After the implementation perceptions related to the targeting, beneficiaries were inquired about the support's appropriateness in terms of adequacy.

**Table 4.6 Beneficiaries Satisfaction in Support Appropriateness**

| *Level of Satisfaction* | *Public Work* | *Direct support* | *Total* |
|---|---|---|---|
| Very Unsatisfied | 17 | 6 | 23 |
| Somehow Unsatisfied | 59 | 14 | 73 |
| Neutral | 9 | 5 | 14 |
| Somehow Satisfied | 186 | 24 | 210 |
| Very Satisfied | 34 | 9 | 43 |
| Total | 305 | 58 | 363 |

*Source:* Own Field Survey, (2020)

According to the survey finding, the majority of both public work and direct support beneficiaries had reported support appropriateness as somehow satisfactory. To stimulate the market, to help lessen dependency on the programme and to motivate savings and investment, cash transfer is highly preferred over food transfers in the PSNP. Although the decision on the mode of transfer depends on other factors and assessments such as closeness of the area to food surplus areas, market/price assessments of food and others, yet the issue of adequacy of transfers particularly, cash transfers have been a matter of debate with respect to their adequacy. In this regards, the adequacy of the transfers, during an interaction in focus groups, discussants indicated that;

> *The amount of cash transfer beneficiaries received even could not cover their meals properly. The transfer did not consider*

*the inflation in food items. The discussants stated that the amount of cash transfer is too little and could not help satisfy their basic needs and this is worsened with reduction of working days.*

According to Yitagesu (2014),66% of respondents prefer food only; food transfer reduces the cost to get food since in the market it is difficult to get the same amount of food if it was cash transfer (Yitagesu, 2014).From the above discussions and findings we can concluded that the UPSNP support is not adequate to meet the basic needs of the beneficiaries. Therefore the amount support should be adjusted and justified based on the current living standard conditions so as to help the beneficiaries to meet their basic necessities.

### *4.2.3 Timeliness of Cash Transfer*

Timely cash transfer of the programme to its beneficiaries was also assessed as it has the power to affect the intended outcomes of the programme if there are deviations from timely transfers of benefits. According to the programme implementation manual wages are transferred to the beneficiaries within 15 days after the end of each month (MoUDH, 2016).

**Table 4.7 Beneficiaries Satisfaction in Timeliness of Cash Transfer**

| *Level of Satisfaction* | *Public Work* | *Direct support* | *Total* |
|---|---|---|---|
| Very Unsatisfied | 8 | 4 | 12 |
| Somehow Unsatisfied | 39 | 17 | 56 |
| Neutral | 6 | 2 | 8 |
| Somehow Satisfied | 210 | 26 | 236 |
| Very Satisfied | 42 | 9 | 51 |
| Total | 305 | 58 | 363 |

*Source:* Own Field Survey, (2020)

As the above table shows the majority of both public work and direct support respondents had described the timeliness of cash transfer as somehow satisfactory. The key informants and the focus groups discussion indicated that at the beginning of the programme payments were not transferred in a timely and regular manner and in accordance with the planned transfer schedules. Delivering benefits timely is one of the principles of UPSNP so as the beneficiaries will not be forced to face worse conditions. When payments are delayed, beneficiaries lose their trust in the programme. Interactions during the FGDs indicate that the timeliness of UPSNP's cash transfer in the study area has been improved as compared to the previous months but sometimes it is delayed. So the obstacles should be assessed and the necessary measure should be taken.

### *4.2.4 Effect of Urban Productive Safety Net Programme*

With regard to the general effects of the programme on the beneficiaries' livelihoods, two options were forwarded to them: negative and positive effect. The survey results showed that, the majority 346(95.3%) respondents reported positive effects whereas 17(4.7%) of the respondents indicated that the programme had negative effects in their livelihoods. When we see in beneficiary type from the total direct support beneficiaries 96.6% are of the view that it brought positive effects while from the total public work beneficiaries 95% brought positive effects on the respondents.

**Table 4.8 Effects of UPSNP**

| *Sex HHH* | *Effects of UPSNP* | | |
|---|---|---|---|
| | *Positive (%)* | *Negative (%)* | *Total (%)* |
| Female | 197(97%) | 6(3%) | 203(100%) |
| Male | 143(93.12%) | 17(6.88%) | 160(100%) |

*Source:* Own Field Survey, (2020)

From the total 203 female headed households, 197(97%) indicated that it brought them positive effects in their livelihoods' and from the total 160 male headed households 149(93.12%) are of the view that the programme has positive effects.

When referring to other study findings, Welteji, et al (2017) found that productive safety net programme in Bale Zone brought positive effects in the overall livelihoods of the beneficiaries, as the majority of the respondents 64.7% revealed that their living standard was improved although 26.4% indicated that it has deteriorated and rest indicated it is the same and some do not know if there are improvements. Gezachew, et al (2017) study result also show that productive safety net programme had significant positive effect on participants in terms of asset building, improvement of food consumption and increased livestock size in the study area and in solving immediate food shortage problems(Gizachew, et al, 2017).

Interactions during the FGDs indicate that UPSNP has a significant positive effect in the livelihoods of beneficiaries. When describing the positive effects of the programme, they stated that the programme gave them a chance to have bank accounts and deposit save some cash on a monthly basis and also to participate in the traditional saving associations like Iquib and Iddir. In addition, it was also indicated that participating in the programme has helped them to become self-confident. They had better social interaction with their neighbors and they participated in different social activities in their community. On the other hand, the programme also strengthened their social networks on which beneficiaries depend on, and helps them in protecting the environment and enhancing working habits of public work beneficiaries.

Of those households who indicated that UPSNP has brought negative impacts on their livelihoods, majority 78.6 % of these beneficiaries indicated that the damage arose as a result of the damaged caused on their previous livelihood sources and their dependency on the programme. In explaining further on how the negative impacts occurred, interviews and focus group discussants indicate that untimely supply of safety materials has brought them health related risks such as bodily injuries among the public work beneficiaries. It was also indicated that safety clothing materials were not provided for the beneficiaries until the first year the programme implementation period.

From the above discussion we can conclude that, UPSNP has positive effects for the majority of the participants and the overall livelihood outcomes of the beneficiaries could be improved if safety materials are provided in a timely fashion. The programme supports the beneficiaries to have additional and stable means of livelihood for them. The programme brought positive effects on their saving culture, in improving their access to food, in strengthening social interactions, in enhancing their working habit and in protecting the environment. The UPSNP has so far enabled beneficiary households to engage in better livelihood activities and to build their assets for better outcomes. On the one hand it is difficult to expect sustainable livelihood outcome from the programme because the amount of cash transfer is not as sufficient to attain sustainable livelihood outcomes. It is also difficult to expect long-term livelihood improvement from the programme as this is not something permanent. By adjusting the amount of cash transfer of the programme, implementing bodies can bring more impact on the livelihoods of beneficiary households for good in the long run as the key informant mentioned during the discussion.

Respondents also responded on whether they have heard about graduation from the programme or not. From the total conditional beneficiary sample households

297(97.4%) respondents forwarded they had information about graduation from the UPSNP whereas, 8 (2.6%) of the respondents have not heard about graduation from the programme.

The survey result also shows that, majority (98.3%) of the respondents know the criteria to identify potential graduates. Out of which,59.9% of the respondents replied that achieving self- sufficiency or self-dependence as a criteria to identify potential graduates, whereas 19.2% indicated increased income from income generating works other than UPSNP transfer as a criteria, 15.6% capacity to feed the household for 12 months as a criteria and 5.0% increased assets as a criteria. On the other hand, 52.5% of the respondent preferred to get loans from the programme whereas the remaining 47.5% of the respondents do not prefer to get loans from the programme. For those who preferred to get loans, the programme can facilitate a chance to engage in different livelihood activities for the betterment of their living condition.

From the total respondents 311(85.7%) of the beneficiaries have received trainings through UPSNP. Out of which, 13.6% received financial trainings, 71.3%trainings in business skills, 11% technical trainings and 4.1% of the respondents had received different life skills trainings. The above discussion indicates that the programme strives to create awareness about the programme and deliver the necessary information for beneficiary households and also tried to build their capacity through specialized trainings.

## 4.3 Contributions of Urban Productive Safety Net Programme

This section presents findings of the contributions of the urban productive safety net programme on the overall livelihoods; discussed covering three major aspects of livelihoods framework. These are (i) Livelihood Assets, (ii) Livelihood Strategies and (iii) Livelihood outcomes and are discussed as follows.

### *4.3.1 Livelihood Assets*

A livelihood involves assets and activities that are required for a means of living. Outcomes of the combination of the assets and activities which are referred to as livelihood results include increased income, increased well-being and reduced vulnerability, improved food security and more sustainable use of natural resources. The assets allow households to generate income, meet their basic needs, manage risk, and cope with stresses and shocks(Sati & Vangchhia, 2017). Accordingly, in this sub-section the major five livelihood assets (Human, Social, Financial, Physical and Natural) are discussed in reference to the contributions of the Urban Productive Safety net Programme.

#### Human Capital

Human capital encompass knowledge expertise, work skills and the physical state of good health and, when combined, helps people to engage with different strategies and achieve their own livelihood goals (UNDP, 2017).The knowledge and capabilities of livelihoods available to individuals that determine how effectively individuals apply their knowledge and capabilities to livelihood activities. Human capital is crucial in order to use other kinds of assets. For this study, the human capital of the sample households is assessed in terms of educational attainments of the household head and health condition of household member's and ability to work.

**Table 4.9 Household Level of Literacy**

| | *Sex of the Household Head* | | *Total* | *Percentage (%)* |
|---|---|---|---|---|
| | *Male* | *Female* | | |
| Unable to read and write | 34 | 78 | 112 | 30.9 |
| Less than 8th grade | 66 | 98 | 164 | 45.2 |
| 9-12 grade | 53 | 26 | 79 | 21.8 |
| TVET or college diploma | 7 | 1 | 8 | 2.2 |
| Degree and above | 0 | 0 | 0 | 0 |
| Total | 160 | 203 | 363 | 100 |

*Source:* Own Field Survey, (2020)

As the survey result shows, the educational attainments of female headed households are far less than that of male counterparts. That mean, female headed beneficiary households comparatively are more vulnerable and prone to poverty than male headed households. Overall, the result shows low literacy level in the study area. Their low level of literacy perhaps might not allow them to engage in a better income generating job this may contribute for their food insecurity.

Another study in Somali region also showed that, in terms of education, large proportions (79.6%) of respondents were illiterate. Due to this, it is not difficult to infer that for significant majority of household heads, their poor educational level might contribute for their food insecurity status. This study result also has similar findings their low level of literacy could not give a chance to engage in better income earning jobs Yitagesu (2014).

## Physical Capital

Physical assets relates to the basic infrastructure and inputs of production needed to support livelihoods (UNDP, 2017). Physical assets in this study are assessed in terms of basic services available in the study area including water supply, health, education and road facility.

**Access to water supply:** beneficiary households in the study area were found to have different types of access to water supply which was from taps found in their living compounds, from public taps and buying from nearby water sources. Concerning the major challenges in their access to water, with the availability of water supply the survey result shows that 209(57.6%) of the sample beneficiary household have problems with water supply in their community whereas, the remaining 154(42.4%) of the respondents did not mention water supply problem in their surroundings. Besides, 45.5% of the households indicated that their problems in terms of access to water is related to the distance 38.4% are related to inadequacy of water taps, 11.4% related to non-functionality of water taps and remaining 4.7% indicated that there are no water supply lines.

From the 363 sample beneficiary households 313(86.2%) of the respondents mentioned UPSNP did not perform any role with related to water supply challenges they are having in their community. This condition forces households to travel long distances to fetch water, which in turn can perhaps affect their livelihood earnings negatively as they tend to spend valuable time and energy for accessing water.

**Health Facility**: the survey results show that majority 347(95.1%) of the households have access to health facilities. Among these, 95.1% have access to nearby health centers not far from their residences, whereas the remaining 4.9% have access to hospitals and private clinics. Moreover, 48.2% of households get free health coverage from the health centers and 13.8% get health assistance by using the support card from the programme. UPSNP in the study area was found to play a significant role in linking beneficiary households with health facilities.

**Educational Facility**: With regard to school facility, majority of the respondents were found to have access to kindergarten, primary and secondary schools nearby to their residences. This indicates that many improvements have been made with regard to access to education as many public schools were opened near to communities in the study area. UPSNP in the study area was found to play a minor role by creating socials linkages with the concerned bodies. That is, 35(9.6%) of the beneficiary households only were linked with free education and they also get educational material support. In line to this, UPSNP does not play any role in relation to the development of educational infrastructure.

**Road Facility**: The study results indicates the roads in the study area were 250(68.9%) paved roads made up of cobble stone, 65(19.7%) were paved road made up of asphalt and the remaining 48(13.2%) were unpaved roads. With respect to the role of UPSNP in connection with road facility, 52.1% of the respondents' indicated that the programme have not yet made any contributions with road facility improvements in their community.

Overall, the contribution of UPSNP in physical assets development is very limited.

## Natural Capital

Natural assets refer to natural resource stocks (soil, water, air, genetic resources, etc.) that can be used as inputs to create additional benefits such as food chains, soil or coastal erosion protection and other natural resources that can support livelihoods(UNDP, 2017). According to Farringiton (2002), natural resources are generally less used in the livelihood strategies of the urban poor, as they tend to be less available, especially in large urban centre(Farrington, 2002).

From the total respondents, 139(38.3%) of the respondents have green area in their house, whereas the remaining 224(61.7%) of the respondents do not have any green area in their house. As stated in UPSNP implementation manual PW component focus on the labor intensive work activities such as urban solid waste management and environmental cleaning, urban beautification and greenery, urban integrated watershed management for the development of community assets and upgrading of social infrastructure.

During an interaction with an expert from Urban Job Creation and Food Security Agency

> *In Dire Dawa city administration terrace, solid waste management, urban greenery, road maintenance and building public latrines are selected activities and undertaken by UPSNP. Dire Dawa faces challenges of periodic floods entering the city which affect people living in slum areas or substandard housings. The terrace done by UPSNP helps to protect those areas from problems of floods. (Urban Job Creation and Food Security Agency expert interview, January 24, 2020 Dire Dawa)*

Public work activities require integrated work through different government bodies for the effective implementation of the programme. The Solid Waste Disposal Municipality, Urban Greenery and Beautification Bureau, and Agriculture Bureau are concerned bodies are involved in public work activities implementation. In this respect, during FGD interactions, UPSNP was found to have a great role in solid waste management of the city administration.

> *Cleaning activities of roads, streets and drainages carried by conditional beneficiaries make the environment to become clean and safe. The cleaning activity is carried out in collaboration with municipality solid waste management and they give technical support for the workers. Trainings are given by the experts to enhance the knowledge and skills of public workers of the programme. Thus the programme contributes to protect the environment from pollution and*

*makes suitable place for the lives of the community. (FGD, February 25, 2020, Dire Dawa)*

The survey result also indicates that majority 47.9% of the beneficiaries believe that UPSNP plays a role in greenery works such as planting grasses and trees, and 25.3% also deem that it also plays a role in conserving existing plants. However, 26.8% of the beneficiaries do not believe that UPSNP is playing a role in urban greenery. During an interview with an expert from Urban Job Creation and Food Security Agency;

*In Dire Dawa city administration Urban Greenery and Beautification Bureau is supporting the programme by giving sites and different technical supports for the tasks of public workers. Nevertheless, there is scarcity of greenery spaces to work within the city. So, the public work activity is often undertaken on works related to reducing floods and increasing of temperature in the city. But there is weak collaboration among the concerned bodies that affect the proper implementation. (Urban Job Creation and Food Security Agency expert interview, January 24, 2020 Dire Dawa)*

In line to this, FGDs interactions indicated that:

*UPSNP in the study area cannot be engaged in development of social infrastructure activities. From areas selected for public work activities building public latrines cannot be done until the third year programme implementation time. In relation with road maintenance, some cobble stone roads were maintained but the activity cannot be done with the required quality and time. The reason for this is lack of coordination and collaboration among the stakeholders and weak commitment among them. (FGD, February 25, 2020, Dire Dawa)*

From the above discussion we can conclude that, protecting the environment can help enhances and protect the livelihoods of the poor and the contribution of UPSNP in this regard is little contributed in urban greenery.

## Financial Capital

Financial assets are financial resources accessible to the family which include access and availability of savings, loans, insurance, remittances, benefits, social welfare cash transfers and value-added property such as livestock and jewellery (Woller, 2011). Income from the sale of labour is often one of the most important assets for the urban poor and one which they tend to prioritize (Farrington, 2002).

Under the UPSNP, beneficiary households receive cash transfers from the programme in Dire Dawa. The transfers and amounts are dependent on the type beneficiary; i.e. public work (conditional transfers) or direct beneficiaries. As indicated 58(16%) of the respondents are direct beneficiaries and got their direct financial support from UPSNP with the gross amount of 215 ETB per month. The remaining majorities who are public work beneficiaries 305(84%) receive conditional benefits after participating in public work activities and the monthly payment from UPSNP is 75 ETB per working day. In addition, majority of the respondents' are beneficiary for three years in UPSNP as per the Programme Implementation Manual, they are allowed to work for a maximum of four days in a month based on a number of beneficiaries in their household. From the cash transfers, the conditional beneficiaries had an obligatory 20% saving until their graduation.

Moreover, beneficiaries participate in different livelihood activities to sustain their households' livelihood. Among the study participants, it was found that 29.5% engage in daily labor, 22.9% in petty trade and 2.2 % in urban agriculture.

In terms of financial support, 23.4% of the programme beneficiaries have received financial support from their relatives, 8.5% from pension, 8.5 % of the respondent from remittance and the remaining 59.6% respondents do not have any financial support.

The financial assets for the sample beneficiary households are conditional and unconditional cash transfer from the programme, income from different livelihood activities (like daily labor, petty trade and urban agriculture), pension and assistance from relatives, and remittance. UPSNP enhances the saving of the beneficiaries all the beneficiaries have bank accounts and also after joining the programme they participate in informal financial institutions these enhance their savings and provides access to loans. Thus the study result indicates UPSNP cash transfer is one of the essential financial sources for the beneficiary households to sustain their lives together with other livelihood activities. Therefore the programme is vital for the households who might not have other sources of income.

## Social Capital

Social assets refers to the social resources on which people can depend while following their livelihood objectives (UNDP, 2017). A social asset refers to networks of mutual support that exist within and between households and communities. Social capital is a valuable and critical resource for poor urban households, especially during times of crisis and socio-economic change (Farrington, 2002).The social assets in the study area were also assessed taking into consideration of the explanations given for social capital.

In addition the beneficiary households had informal relations in their communities to strengthen their social linkage. The qualitative data result indicated after joining UPSNP beneficiary households are participating more in informal organizations like iddir and iquib and they got financial and social support from their communities in times of crisis and the cash transfer helps to develop their confidence to participate in different social activities in their communities. So as a result of being beneficiary in the programme their participation in formal and informal institutions increased and also the communities develop trust among them. Therefore UPSNP helps the beneficiary households to strengthen their social network within the communities.

This study finding indicates UPSNP contribute the improvements of households' livelihood assets in the study area. In this regards, different studies have indicated the contribution of productive safety net programme for the households' livelihoods. For instance, Welteji et al (2017) PSNP in Bale Zone prevents asset depletion, in enhancing road constructions, natural resource conservation soil conservation through soil and stone bund, and check dams' construction. These all community-based infrastructures were helping the livelihood of the community asset accumulation, and development of the local community (Welteji et al., 2017). Ali ( 2011) also in his study in the rural parts of Ethiopia indicated that PSNP reduces asset holding of beneficiary households compared to non-beneficiary households(Ali, 2011).

### *4.3.2 Livelihood Strategies*

Livelihood strategies are the planned activities that people undertake to build their livelihoods basing on the assets they have. Livelihood strategies include coping strategies designed to respond to shocks in the short term, and adaptive strategies designed to improve circumstances in the long term. Livelihood strategies are determined by the assets and opportunities available (Farrington, 2002).These livelihood strategies lead straight to livelihood outcomes.

In this respect, the survey results of this study indicate that beneficiary households participate in different livelihood activities to sustain their lives. From the total beneficiary households 43.6% of the respondents depend on UPSNP cash transfer to sustain their lives and the remaining 56.4% of the respondents made their livelihoods using additional source of income to complement UPSNP cash transfers.

**Table 4.10 Respondents' Means of Livelihoods**

| *Sex of HHH* | *Beneficiary type* | | *Livelihood activities* | | | | |
|---|---|---|---|---|---|---|---|
| | | *Only DS from UPSNP* | *Only payment PW from USNP* | *Daily labor* | *Petty trade* | *Urban agriculture* | *Total* |
| Male | PW | 0 | 49 | 65 | 25 | 2 | 141 |
| | DS | 18 | 0 | 0 | 0 | 0 | 18 |
| | Total | 18 | 49 | 65 | 25 | 2 | 159 |
| Female | PW | 0 | 57 | 42 | 62 | 3 | 164 |
| | DS | 36 | 0 | 0 | 1 | 3 | 40 |
| | Total | 36 | 57 | 42 | 63 | 6 | 204 |

*Source:* Own Field Survey, (2020)

The above table shows that the majority of direct support beneficiaries do not engage in other livelihood activities and their major sources of income is UPSNP cash transfer. Besides, most of female headed households participated in petty trade and male headed households participated in daily labour which can show the gendered division of labor by occupation. The survey result indicates that more than half of public work beneficiary households participate in other means of income in addition to the cash transfers they are getting from UPSNP.

A study undertaken by Degefa, (2008) in understanding the realities of urban poor and their food security situation in Addis Ababa, he indicated that the urban poor get earnings for their livelihoods by engaging in a variety of low pay employment jobs, causal work and wage labor, and diverse informal activities as a result of low education they had.

The earnings they make are very low to meet the basic needs of their family members and this keeps these individuals and households in poverty trap (Degefa, 2008).

Based on the above discussions, it is possible to conclude that UPSNP cash transfer in the study area is playing a major role as a source of income for the beneficiary households in times of stresses and shock. It has a significant importance for the households who do not have other means of income to sustain their livelihoods. So UPSNP offer supplementary and secure source of income for the households in the study area.

### *4.3.3 Livelihood Outcomes*

UPSNP is designed as an intervention for the betterment of beneficiary households' livelihood strategies in order to bring sustainable improvements to their lives. In this regards, the study has assessed the outcomes brought on beneficiary households as a result of the UPSNP. The assessment here is done basing on beneficiaries' income status and food access in the study area.

#### Income Sources

The beneficiaries had different source of income for their livelihoods. The means of their income is from urban productive safety net programme, financial assistance from pension, relatives and remittance. Their monthly income estimated from the above sources.

Income sources as aforementioned above among the beneficiary households is made up of different sources ranging from cash transfers from the programme to financial assistances through pensions, supports from relatives and remittances. Accordingly in the assessment, income is estimated from these sources.

The number of direct support beneficiaries per household receiving cash transfers ranges from one to four with a monthly amount of 215, 430, 615 and 860 ETB per number of beneficiary in the household respectively on monthly basis. From the total 363 sample households respondents, 305(84%) were participating in public work activities and receive 75 ETB calculated by the number of days labor and number of beneficiaries in the household. while the remaining 58 (16%) were receiving unconditional cash transfers from UPSNP with an amount of 215 ETB per month. The survey result showed that from the total 305 beneficiaries 203(66.6%) of the households had four beneficiary members and this shows majority of public work beneficiaries had the maximum number of beneficiary members in their household, whereas from the total 58 direct support beneficiary 25(43.1%) had two beneficiary per household and 21(36.2%) had three beneficiary per household. This indicates public work beneficiaries have more beneficiary members in their household than direct support beneficiaries.

**Table 4.11 No of UPSNP Beneficiaries in the Household**

| *Sex of HHH* | *Beneficiary type* | *No of beneficiary per HH* | | | | |
|---|---|---|---|---|---|---|
| | | *One* | *Two* | *Three* | *Four* | *Total* |
| Male | PW | 0 | 3 | 41 | 97 | 141 |
| | DS | 2 | 6 | 8 | 3 | 19 |
| | Total | 2 | 9 | 49 | 100 | 160 |
| Female | PW | 6 | 15 | 37 | 106 | 164 |
| | DS | 2 | 19 | 13 | 5 | 39 |
| | Total | 8 | 34 | 50 | 111 | 203 |

*Source:* Own Computation, (2020)

The above table indicates public work female headed household are having greater number of members of household than female headed households. In line to this, the total monthly estimated income of the respondent households was a minimum of 200 ETB and a maximum of 3400 ETB and the average monthly income was 1180 ETB.

The average monthly income of direct support beneficiaries was 480 ETB and 880 ETB was average monthly income the public work beneficiaries. The minimum monthly income of the household indicates households do not have other sources of income other than UPSNP cash transfer. On the one hand the high income range shows that the household engage in different livelihood activities other than the programme cash transfer.

The qualitative data result shows that the UPSNP has brought additional source of income that complements incomes from other livelihood activities beneficiary household engage. As per the results, after joining the programme, there is a change in the monthly income of beneficiary households. As the cash transfer is stable sources of income households get credits from their neighbors that the programme gives guaranty for repayment of loans if taken .But as repeatedly indicated, it is difficult to sustain their lives with the transfer amounts provided from UPSNP. The amount of cash transfer did not consider the current living standard conditions and it is too small to satisfy their basic needs. Therefore there is a need to adjust the amount of cash transfer taking into consideration of the current urban living conditions so as to help beneficiary households and to achieve the intended outcomes of the programme.

**Table 4.12 Major Expenses of the Household**

| *Expenses* | *Frequency* | *Percentage (%)* |
|---|---|---|
| Food | 347 | 95.6 |
| Education | 1 | 0.3 |
| Medical | 4 | 1.1 |
| House rent | 5 | 1.4 |
| Water and electric fees | 1 | 0.3 |
| Loan repayments | 5 | 1.4 |
| Total | 363 | 100 |

*Source:* Own Computation, (2020)

The survey result the majority of the public work respondents mentioned the major expenses of the household were food 347(95.6%) and the direct support respondents mentioned 56(96.55%) of the respondents their major expense were food. Food cost which is a basic necessity is taking the larger share of the expenditures of the household. This can hinder these beneficiary households from participating in additional income source activities as the chance to save and make investments is limited.

According to UPSNP Implementation Manual each conditional beneficiary household has an obligatory saving of 20% which cannot be withdrawn until their graduation (MoUDH, 2016). That is, all the beneficiary households had saving in their bank account. Despite involvement in one or combination of some (permanent employment, casual jobs, wage labor and informal activities), the income people draw can neither meet the basic needs nor to save some amount out of those jobs (Degefa, 2008). In this regards, focus group discussants value the saving initiative attribute of the programme because it had given a bright future for the beneficiary households. The saving initiated beneficiaries to engage in different livelihood activities to make more income and to save more for their future. As the survey result indicate most of sample beneficiaries have been beneficiaries of the programme for three years in UPSNP and are expected graduate from the programme in this year. In this regards, it was found that they are getting different livelihood trainings to become self-employed or employed in better paying jobs. Accordingly they indicated that they are waiting for the grant from the programme, together with the savings they had which can help them to become self-reliant. Potential graduates select the area they want to engage in but they rose as a complaint that the grant is not being transferred in accordance with the planned transfer schedule which makes them lose their trust and create fear among the beneficiaries. The saving initiative encourages beneficiaries saving culture and also initiates them to engage in different livelihood activities and become savers.

With regards to other sources of income, majority 73.6% of the respondents did not get any assistance from any other source than UPSNP cash transfer. This indicates the programme cash transfer stands as a sole source of income for these beneficiary households and helps as an additional source of income to sustain their livelihoods.

The survey findings also revealed that, cash transfer received by most of the beneficiaries 359(98.9%) from the programme only fulfills households' food demand for less than a month. This result also corroborates with the qualitative findings aforementioned that the cash transfer they are receiving is too small to cover their basic need costs.

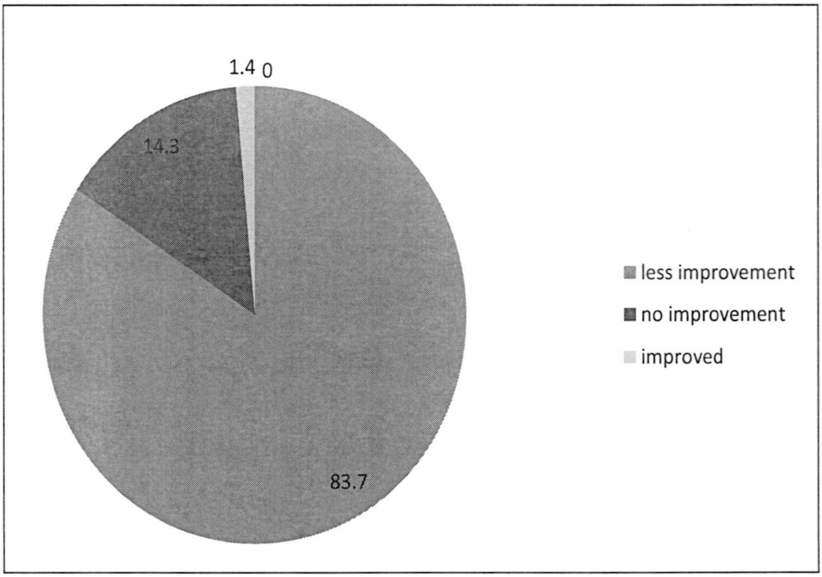


*Source:* Own Computation, (2020)

*Figure 4.2: Income Status of the HH after joining UPSNP*

The above figure shows that among majority beneficiaries (83.7%), after they joined the programme their income has shown less improvement. The remaining 52(14.3%) indicated that it has improved and only seven beneficiaries (1.9%) were of the view that there is no improvements at all in their incomes. This can show that the cash transfer received from the programme though small and insufficient, yet it is contributing in improving the incomes of beneficiary households.

## Food Access Conditions of Beneficiary Households

Food access refers to individuals having adequate assets or incomes to produce, buy or purchase adequate foods needed to maintain adequate diet/nutrition level (Woller, 2011). According to Farrington (2002), urban economies are characterized by a greater degree of commercialization, and most basic goods such as food and accommodation must be bought or rented through the market. Food access is largely

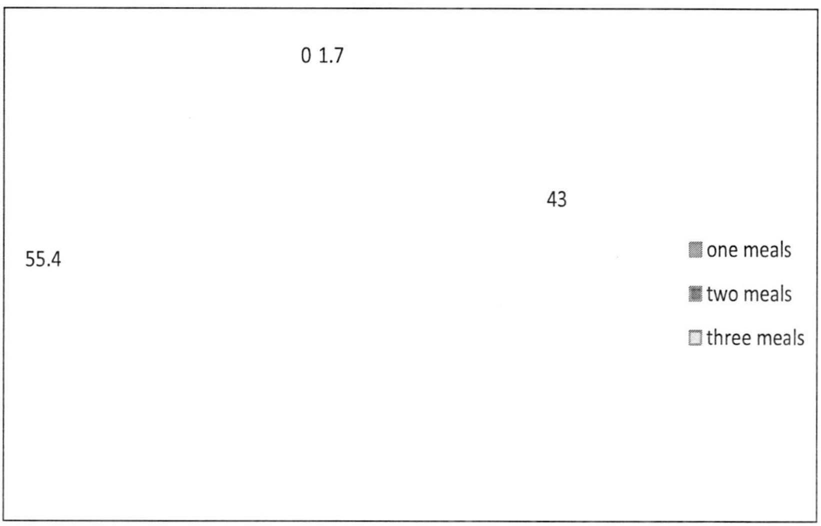


*Source:* Own Computation, (2020)

*Figure 4.3 Households Number of Meals Taken Per Day.*

related to household income and own production. Level of household income, expenditure, markets and prices determine the level of food access.

Apart from the assessment over income as a result of the UPSNP, the study has also assessed if there are improvements in food access of beneficiary households

Concerning the number of meals taken per day, 201(55.4%) of the beneficiary households had three meals per day, 156(43%) had two meals per day and 6(1.7%) had one meal per day. From the total respondents' 353(97.2%) forwarded that UPSNP has contributed in improving their household to have access to enhanced number of meals per day.

**Table 4.13 Beneficiary Type and the Food Access Status**

| | | *Food access status (Meals)* | | | *Chi-square(p)* |
|---|---|---|---|---|---|
| | | *One* | *Two* | *Three* | |
| Beneficiary type | PW | 6 | 122 | 177 | 0.16 |
| | DS | 0 | 34 | 23 | |
| | Total | 6 | 156 | 200 | |
| Family size | Less than three | 3 | 106 | 138 | 0.000 |
| | Four and more than four | 3 | 50 | 63 | |
| | Total | 6 | 156 | 201 | |

*Source:* Own Computation, (2020)

The results in the above table show that there is no significant difference between the two categories of beneficiaries, although the case was different coming to the family size. The result indicates that there is a significant relationship between access to food and family size.

In similar lines, focus group discussants have explained the contribution of UPSNP to households' food access as follows;

*The cash transfer of the UPSNP gives the opportunity to buy food items for the beneficiaries. There is an increase in the*

> *number of meals and the quantity and quality of meals taken per day. They got a chance to eat a variety of food items. (FGD, February 25, 2020, Dire Dawa)*

With regard to the extent improvement on households' food access after joining UPSNP, there was somehow improvement for 305(84%) respondents, there was improvement for 50(13.8%) respondents and for 1 (0.3%) household, and there was a significant improvement.

Different studies have reflected the contribution of safety net programme in improving the food access of beneficiaries. For instance, PSNP in Bale Zone had increased the number of dining times and the amount of meal and food at each dining time. The program has also increased the food expenditure and level of consumption. By keeping the minimum level and smoothing consumption, PSNP has improved the food security status of the beneficiary households (Welteji et al., 2017). Similarly, a study on the contribution of PSNP in Babile District indicated that participant households were more likely to be food secure comparing to non-participant households. In similar lines PSNP had significantly increased household calorie intake (Badassa, 2018) and there were improvements in number of meals taken and food access status of beneficiaries' households Yitagesu (2014).

From the above discussions it can be concluded that, UPSNP cash transfer has some contribution in the number of meals per day and the amount of meals taken by the households. However, as was found monthly cash transfer of the programme does not fulfill households' food demand for a full month and this show that the inadequate amount of cash transfer to beneficiaries which does not take into consideration of market prices could limit their food access.

## 4.4 Challenges in the Implementation of UPSNP

According to the survey result, 295(81.3%) of the respondents mentioned beneficiary households who do not fulfill the criteria are not be included in the programme whereas, the remaining 68(18.7%) respondents forwarded households who are not eligible have been included in the programme. This result in general shows that the targeting though not comprehensively is in compliance with the implantation targets.

From conditional sample beneficiaries 92.5% of the respondents' responded children' less than 18 years in their household do not participate in public work activities and also pregnant or lactating women are exempted from participating in public work activities. From the total respondents' 95.1% responded that they have not seen a pregnant or lactating women participating in public work activities. This indicates that public work activity is being implemented in accordance with the programme implementation manual.

### Implementation Arrangements and Compliance with PIM

The programme implementation manual shows how to appeal when beneficiaries face unjust and unfair treatments from UPSNP. Accordingly majority of the respondents 324(89.3%) indicated that when they face unfair treatments they complain for Kebele appeals committee, 32(8.8%) complain during community meeting and the remaining mentioned give their complaints for their team leaders and for Kebele UPSNP coordinators. The key informant interview with Urban Job Creation and Food Security Agency and Labour and Social Affair Bureau experts revealed that there is a structure for appeal mechanisms when beneficiaries face different unfair treatments where they can raise their complaints for Kebele appeals committees.

The committees are expected to give immediate responses on the appeals as soon as possible. This shows in the study area there is structure for complaints and appeals mechanism in place. Lack of mechanisms for appeal thus is not a challenge in the overall implementation the programme effectively in the study area.

Different studies have reflected challenges for implementation of productive safety net programme. For instance PSNP practice in Bale Zone was challenged by a lack of monitoring and evaluation of structures, low payment and limited awareness of beneficiaries (Welteji et al., 2017). According to Teshome (2013), some of the challenges of the programme were in targeting of beneficiaries and inability to distinguish between acute and chronic food insecurity at grassroots level, application of single wage rate at national level, lack of the capacity to manage, unprecedented amount of cash flowing into the district and linkage problem at grassroots level (Teshome, 2013).

**Table 4.14 Challenges in the Urban Productive Safety Net Programme Implementation**

| *Challenges* | *Frequency* | *Percentage (%)* |
|---|---|---|
| Lack of strong institutionalized mechanism for appeal | 25 | 6.9 |
| Lack of transparency and accountability | 55 | 15.2 |
| Low community participation | 37 | 10.2 |
| Poor coordination across government offices | 122 | 33.6 |
| Delay of paymentsor transfers | 93 | 25.6 |
| Fear of graduation | 21 | 5.8 |
| Others(no institutional implementation challenges) | 10 | 2.8 |
| Total | 363 | 100 |

*Source:* Own Field Survey, (2020)

From the total respondents 122(33.6%) mentioned poor coordination across government offices, 93(25.6%) delays in payment of transfers, and 55(15.2%) lack of transparency and accountability are the major three challenges in the implementation of UPSNP mentioned by the respondents.

During interaction in the FGDs about related challenges, it was indicated that;

> *The main challenge to the implementation of the programme is lack of commitment among government officials, delay of payment of transfers, the amount of cash transfer is not sufficient to address basic needs and lack of follow up by experts in the activities undertaken by public workers. (FGD, February 25, 2020, Dire Dawa)*

Effective implementation of UPSNP requires coordination among different concerned bodies. The key informants boldly explained weak coordination and collaboration among stakeholders which affects the effective implementation of the programme. In Dire Dawa city administration, different selected public work activities and linking the beneficiary households to different social services could not be done within the required manner due to lack of coordination among concerned bodies. The amount of cash transfer is also another challenge that needs to be addressed.

From the above discussions it can be concluded that in the study area weak coordination among stakeholders, weak commitment among government officials, and low amount of cash transfer and delay of transfer of payments the major challenges which are hindering the effective implementation of the programme.

Chapter Five

# Conclusions and Recommendations

## 5.1 Conclusions

Urban Productive Safety Net Programme (UPSNP) has been implemented as a pilot project in Dire Dawa City Administration. In this respect, this study has tried to assess the roles that are played by this programme in improving the conditions of urban dwellers in Dire Dawa City between 2017 and 2019. From the city administration, three Kebeles were selected and 363 households were included as participants of the study. This research specifically has assessed the role of UPSNP in improving the beneficiary households' livelihood status, status food access and challenges of programme implementation.

In the study area, majority of the respondents were female headed and they were also the one with lower level of literacy. Their low educational level hinders them from participating in high paying jobs; and due to this they engage in low paid jobs to sustain their livelihoods. From the study participants, 84% of sample are participating and benefiting from public work component and the remaining 16% are benefiting from the direct support component.

The following concluding remarks are drawn from the analysis made in the previous chapter;

- The targeting of beneficiaries in the city has been limited in targeting and benefiting households who are poor due to quota targeting. Besides, the cash transfers given to the targeted beneficiaries were found to be too small to fulfill the basic needs of the poor.
- UPSNP in Dire Dawa city has improved saving cultures, serves as additional and stable sources of income for the beneficiaries, helps for covering part of their food expenditures, strengthened social networks, helped to protect the environment and has enhanced the working habit of the beneficiaries.
- The programmes involvement in terrace development and urban greenery activity is helping the city as a protection against floods and in reducing the increasing temperature in the city. Besides, environmental cleaning activity which is part of the UPSNP is contributing to protect the environment from pollution and is creating healthy environment for the communities.
- Apart from the contribution of the programme as an income sources, it is also contributing in enhancing access to food in terms of improving the number of meals per day and the quality of meals taken per day.
- The major challenges indicated were weak coordination among stakeholders, weak commitment among government officials and low amount of cash transfer and delay of transfer of payments which are hindering the proper and effective implementation of the programme.

## 5.2 Recommendations

The following recommendations are suggested as a means of improving the effectiveness of the UPSNP basing on the concluding remarks above;

- The inadequacy of cash transfer to satisfy the basic needs of the beneficiary households have been raised as a major dilemma of the programme. Thus, it is necessary to reconsider the amount of cash transfers and has to be adjusted in such a way that can meet the basic need costs of beneficiaries.
- It is also recommended that programme implementers conduct market price and availability of well-functioning market objective assessments so as to dispense matching benefits with the current living standards
- If this is not the case, it is very pertinent to consider provisioning of food transfers in place of cash transfers so as to compensate the inadequacies in transfer amounts.
- Effective implementation of UPSNP requires coordination among different concerned bodies, although this was not the case in the study area. Therefore, it very crucial that Urban Job Creation and Food Security Agency and Labor and Social Affairs Bureau strengthen their coordination with other concerned bodies for an effective implementation of the programme.
- Another drawback duly noted of the programme Dire Dawa City Administration is the quota targeting. That is, as a result of the quota targeting, those who are poor and who could have been benefited from the programme are not being targeted as a result of

the quota. Thus, policy wise it is pertinent to assess the quota targeting criteria that had brought significant exclusion of poor households as no one should be left behind in despair.

- Regional and local level finance offices should improve timely transfer of resources to beneficiaries by avoiding the fragmentation across PSNP payment implementing institutions and following regional and kebele annual safety net plans.

# Reference


Ali, H. (2011). *School of Graduate Studies Impacts of Productive Safety Net Program on Household Welfare and Labour Supply in Rural Ethiopia/: A Panel Data Approach Habtamu Ali Beshir A thesis submitted to the school of graduate studies of Addis Ababa University in the p.*

Ani, F. dkk. (2017). Applying Empowerment Approach In Community Development. *Journal University Tun Hussein Onn Malaysia, Johor, Malaysia*, (November), 506–508. Retrieved from https://jurnal.umj.ac.id/index.php/icss/article/view/2359

Badassa Wolteji Chala, M. T. C. (2018). *Impact of Productive Safety Net Programme on Food Security/: The Case of Impact of Productive Safety Net Programme on Food Security/: The Case of Babile District, Somali Regional State, Ethiopia*. (June 2019).

Baker, J., & Schuler, N. (2004). Analyzing urban poverty: A summary of methods and approaches. *World Bank Policy Research Working Paper No. 3399*, (April), 1–66. https://doi.org/10.1177/0956247808096115

Bank, A. D. (2014). Urban poverty in Asia. In *Finance and Development* (Vol. 44). https://doi.org/10.1177/0169796X0602300213

Burchi, F., & Muro, P. De. (2012). A human development and capability approach to food security: Conceptual framework and informational basis. *United Nations Development Programme*, (February), 1(1): 46.

CSA. (2016). *Ethiopia Demographic and Health Survey*.

CSA. (2018). *THE 2015/16 ETHIOPIAN HOUSEHOLD CONSUMPTION – EXPENDITURE (HCE) SURVEY RESULTS*.

CSA and WFP. (2014). *Ethiopia Comprehensive Food Security and Vulnerability Analysis (CFSVA)*. (March).

DDAC. (2014). *Resettlement Action Plan*. (December).

Degefa Tolosa. (2008). *Understanding the Realities of Urban Poor and their Food Security Situations:A Case Study at Berta Gibi and Gemahu Safar in Addis Ababa City < Ethiopia*.

Devereux, S., Sabates-wheeler, R., Taye, M. T., Sabates, R., & Sima, F. (2014). *Graduation from the Food Security Programme in Ethiopia/: FAC Ethiopia Final Report*. (March).

Eneyew, A., & Bekele, W. (2012). *Causes of household food insecurity in Wolayta/:Southern Ethiopia. 3*(3), 35–48. https://doi.org/10.5897/JSPPR11.069

FAO. (2003). *TRADE REFORMS AND FOOD SECURITY conceptualizing the linkages.*

FAO, UNICEF, WFP, & Save the Children. (2009). *Emergency Food Security Assessment*. 68–70.

Farrington, J. (2002). *Livelihoods Approaches in Urban Areas/: General Lessons, with Illustrations from Indian Cases.*

Fernandes, E. (2007). Urban Land Regularization Programs: State of Knowledge. In *Global Urban Poverty Setting the Agenda*. Retrieved from www.wilsoncenter.org

Gezimu, G. (2012). *DETERMINANTS OF FOOD INSECURITY AMONG HOUSEHOLDS IN ADDIS ABABA CITY, ETHIOPIA. 10*(2), 159–173.

Gizachew Dessalegn, Dr. ponguru CS Reddy, D. H. B. (2017). *International Journal of Economics And Business Management Impact of Productive Safety Net Programme on Household Asset and Livelihood Building of Farm Household the Case of Laygayint District Ambhara Regional State South Gondar Administrative Zone, Ethiopi.* (October).

Hagos, Y. (2014). *The Economic Impact of Productive Safety Net Program on Poverty/: Evidence from Central Zone of Tigrai National Regional State, Ethiopia Abstract/: 3*(4), 426–436.

Jha, S., Kotwal, A., & Ramaswami, B. (2013). Safety nets and food programs in Asia: A comparative perspective. *ADB Economics Working Paper Series, 371*(371), 1–26. https://doi.org/10.2139/ssrn.2322639

Krantz, L. (2001). The sustainable livelihood approach to poverty reduction: An introduction. *Swedish International Development Policy*, (Division for Policy and Socio-Economic A Naalysis), 1–40.

Marston, A., & Grady, H. (2014). *Tackling Ultra-poverty through the Graduation Approach/: Situating Sustainable Livelihoods in the Landscape of Social Protection and Safety Nets Ama Marston and Heather Grady Contact Information/: Contents.* (March), 1–33.

MOLSA. (2014). *National Social Protection Policy of Ethiopia. Federal Democratic Republic of Ethiopia.*

MoUDH. (2016). *Urban Productive Safety Net Program Implementation Manual.*

MoUHD. (2015). *Urban Productive Safety Net Project Appraisal Document (PAD).*

Nations, U. (2019). *World Population Prospects.*

Sati, V. P., & Vangchhia, L. (2017). *A Sustainable Livelihood Approach to Poverty Reduction: An Empirical Analysis of Mizoram, the Eastern Extension of the Himalaya*. https://doi.org/10.1007/978-3-319-45623-2

Sen, A. (1982). Poverty and Famines An Essay on Entitlement and Deprivation. In *Oxford, Clarendon Press*.

Sepúlveda, M., & Nyst, C. (2012). The Human Rights approach to Social Protection. In *Ministry for Foreign Affairs of Finland*. Retrieved from http://ssrn.com/abstract=2114384

Teshome. (2013). *challenges of implementing the productive net programme*. 0–40.

UN Habitat. (2008). *Ethiopia/: Dire Dawa Urban Profile*. Retrieved from http://www.humanitarianlibrary.org/sites/default/files/2013/07/2740_alt.pdf

UNDP. (2017). *Application of the Sustainable Livelihoods Framework in Development Projects*. 1–22. Retrieved from www.latinamerica.undp.org

UNDP. (2018). *Industrialization with a Human Face*. 108. Retrieved from http://hdr.undp.org/sites/default/files/ethiopia_national_human_development_report_2018.pdf

UNDP Ethiopia. (2018). Ethiopia ' s Progress Towards Eradicating Poverty. *Implementation of the Third United Nations Decade for the Eradication of Poverty (2018 – 2027)*, 1–9.

WB. (1996). *History of Social Safety Nets at the World Bank*. 85–160.

Welteji, D., Mohammed, K., & Hussein, K. (2017). The contribution of Productive Safety Net Program for food security of the rural households in the case of Bale Zone, Southeast Ethiopia. *Agriculture & Food Security*, 1–11. https://doi.org/10.1186/s40066-017-0126-4

Woller, G. (2011). LIVELIHOOD & FOOD SECURITY CONCEPTUAL FRAMEWORK LIFT – Livelihood and Food Security Technical Assistance. *Usaid*, 36.

Wondim, A. K. (2018). Impact of productive safety net program in rural community of Ethiopia: A review study. *Journal of Agricultural Extension and Rural Development*, *10*(5), 84–88. https://doi.org/10.5897/jaerd2018.0952

World Bank. (2013). *Ethiopia's Productive Safety Net Program ( PSNP ) Integrating Disaster And Climate Risk Management: Case study. Building resilience*. (1), 19. Retrieved from http://documents.worldbank.org/curated/en/2013/06/18142388 4500/Rendered/PDF/806220WP0P12680Box0379812B00PUBLIC0.pdf

Yitagesu Fikadu. (2014). *Impact of Productive Safety Net Programme on Food Security in Ethiopian Somali Region: The Case of Kebereibeyah woreda*.

# List of Acronyms

| | | |
|---|---|---|
| CE | : | Citizens Engagement |
| CSA | : | Central statistics agency |
| DDAC | : | Dire Dawa Administration Council |
| DFID | : | Department for International Development |
| DS | : | Direct Support |
| FAO | : | Food and Agriculture organization |
| FGD | : | Focus Group Discussion |
| FM | : | Financial Management |
| GOE | : | Government of Ethiopia |
| HH | : | Household |
| HHH | : | Household Head |
| HICE | : | Household Income, Consumption and Expenditure |
| ILO | : | International Labor Organization |
| IMF | : | International Monetary Fund |
| KII | : | Key Informant Interview |
| MIS | : | Management Information System |
| MOLSA | : | Ministry of Labor and Social Affair |
| MoUDH | : | Ministry of Urban Development and Housing |
| PIM | : | Programme Implementation Manual |
| PPS | : | Probability Proportional to Size |
| PSNP | : | Productive Safety Net Programme |

| | |
|---|---|
| PW | : Public Work |
| SL | : Sustainable Livelihood |
| SLF | : Sustainable Livelihood Framework |
| SNNPR | : Southern Nation, Nations and Nationalities Peoples region |
| SPSS | : Statistical Package for Social Science |
| SSN | : Social Safety nets |
| UPSNP | : Urban Productive Safety Net Programme |
| UN | : United Nations |
| UNCED | : United Nations Conference on Environment and Development |
| UNDP | : United Nations Development Programme |
| USAID | : United States Agency for International Development |
| WB | : World Bank |
| WFP | : World Food Programme |

# Index


A

Adama, 30
Adama (Oromia), 15
Addis Ababa, 15, 30, 47
Agriculture Bureau, 74
Asayita, 30
Asosa, 30
Asosa (Benshangul), 15
Assaita (Afar), 15
Asset ownership, 41
Average monthly income, 81

B

Babile District, 87
Bale Zone, 87, 89
Bale Zone Saweyna Woreda, 63
Bangladesh, 13, 40
Basic Need Approach, 36
Basic sanitation, 27
Beautification Bureau, 74
Beneficiary Households, 85
Brundtland Commission, 38
Build skills and experience, 38
Bureau of Labour and Social Affairs, 52

C

Capacity and potential, 38
Cash transfer, 87
Cash transfers, 79
Casual jobs, 83
Catholics, 57
Causal work and wage labor, 79
Chronic food insecurity, 89
City Administration, 20, 50
Community affairs, 33
Components of Food Security, 25
Conceptual Framework of the Study, 42
Conditional beneficiaries, 57
Conditional Cash Transfers, 31
Consumption and Expenditure, 28

D

Data Collection Methods, 51
Department for International Development, 42
Dessie, 30
Dessie (Amhara), 15
Development of Livelihoods, 33
Development programme, 13
Dire Dawa, 15, 17, 19, 28, 30
Dire Dawa Administration, 17, 47
Dire Dawa City, 20, 46, 49, 92, 93
Dire Dawa City Administration, 16, 19, 20, 45, 90, 91
Direct support beneficiaries, 56

E

Ecosystems, 25
Educational Facility, 72

Educational status, 55
Entitlement approach, 36
Environmental degradation, 27
Environmental protection, 43
Epidemics, 36
Ethical Considerations, 21
Ethiopia, 13, 17
Ethiopian Government, 18
Ethiopian National Social Protection Policy, 15
Ethiopia's Productive Safety Net Programme, 15
Extreme Poverty, 36

F

Families in low-wage employment, 29
Families in marginal self-employment, 29
Family size of the household, 59
Famine mortality, 36
Female headed households, 66
Financial Capital, 24, 25, 39, 76
Financial Support, 33
Focus Group Discussion, 48, 49, 52
Food access, 26, 85
Food Access Conditions, 85
Food and Agriculture Organization, 26
Food and family size, 86
Food availability, 26
Food safety, 43
Food Security, 25, 41
Food Security Agency, 52, 74, 75, 88, 93
Food Security Programme, 18
Food stability, 26
Food utilization, 26
Forestry, 25
Functional literacy classes, 33
Future skills, 39

G

Gambella, 30
Gambella (Gambella), 15
Genetic resources, 25
Government of Ethiopia, 29
Green area, 73

H

Harar (Harari), 15
Harari, 30
Hawassa, 30
Health and education, 18
Health and education facilities, 28
Health Facility, 72
Health status, 24
Household assets, 43
Household Consumption Expenditure Survey, 14
Household Income, 28
Human Capital, 24, 39, 70

I

Income generation, 41
Income Sources, 80
Institutional Strengthening, 31
International Labor Organization, 36
International Monetary Fund, 14

J

Jigjiga, 30
Jigjiga (Somali), 15
Job Creation Offices, 49

K

Key Informant Interview, 48, 51

L

Lack of manpower, 35
Latin America, 14
Livelihood and Livelihood Capitals, 23
Livelihood Assets, 70
Livelihood framework, 39
Livelihood Outcomes, 70, 80
Livelihood Services, 31
Livelihood Strategies, 70, 78
Livelihoods and betterment, 17
Livelihoods improvement, 16
Low-quality jobs, 28

M

Man-made hazards, 18
Marginal self-employment, 28
Marital status, 55
Medicine accessibility, 40
Mekele, 30
Mekele (Tigray), 16
Mexican crisis, 14

N

National Food Security programme, 30
National poverty, 28
National Rural Employment Guarantee Act, 14
National social safety net, 29
Natural assets, 25, 43
Natural Capital, 25, 39, 73
Natural resource, 73
Negative impacts, 68
Non-beneficiaries, 34

P

Permanent employment, 83
Physical assets, 43
Physical capital, 25, 39
Poverty alleviation, 41
Poverty and starvation, 36
Practical approach, 38
Primary and secondary education, 58
Productive Safety Net Programme, 15, 29, 40, 41
Productive Safety Nets Plan, 30
Programme implementation manual, 88
Project Management and Coordination, 31
Protection against floods, 92
Protestant, 57
Public work activity, 88
Public Work beneficiaries, 50

Q

Qualitative approach, 48
Qualitative data, 77
Qualitative Data Analysis, 53
Qualitative Data Collection, 51
Quantitative approach, 48
Quantitative Data Analysis, 52
Quantitative Data Collection, 51

R

Remote areas, 35
Road Facility, 73
Rural Ethiopia, 28
Rural parts of Ethiopia, 63
Rural poverty, 27
Rural to urban migration, 17

S

Safety Net Support, 31
Scope and Limitations of the Study, 20
Skills and work habits, 43
Social Affair Bureau, 88
Social Capital, 24, 39, 77
Social safety net, 40
Social Safety Nets Programmes, 40
Socio Economic Condition, 47
Solid Waste Disposal, 74
Starvation deaths, 36
Statistical Packages for Social Science, 52
Sub Saharan African region, 14
Survey result, 83

T

Tequila crisis, 14
Theoretical Framework, 35
Trade and industry, 47
Transfer of payments, 92
Transparency and accountability, 37

U

UN Universal Declaration of Human Rights, 37
Unconditional Cash Transfers, 31
United Nations, 26
United Nations population, 47
Urban Food Security, 49
Urban Food Security Strategy, 18
Urban Greenery, 74
Urban households, 59
Urban Job Creation, 18, 52, 74, 75, 88
Urban Job Creation and Food Security Agency, 63
Urban population, 27, 29
Urban poverty, 27, 28
Urban Productive Safety Net Programme, 15, 19, 20, 29, 43, 52, 56, 61, 66, 69, 91
Urban safety, 41
Urban settlements in poverty, 42

V

Vicious circle of poverty, 58

W

Wage labor, 83
Watershed management, 34
Weak commitment, 92
Welfare Monitoring Survey, 28
World Bank, 14, 16, 30
World Food Summit, 26

Y

Yamane, 49